Daniel and Jill –
Blessings!

REVIVAL

REVIVED!

The 1995 Brownwood, Texas,
Revival
and Its Enduring Impact

20th Anniversary Edition

JOHN AVANT
& ALVIN L. REID
EDITORS

Eph 3:20,21

©2015 by John Avant and Alvin L. Reid. Gospel Advance Books. Originally published © *1996 by J. Avant, M. McDow, A. Reid by Broadman & Holman Publishers, Nashville, Tennessee.*

Dewey Decimal Classification: 269.2
Subject Heading: Revivals \ Evangelism
Library of Congress Card Catalog Number: 95-22937
Unless otherwise noted, Scripture quotations are from the New King James Version, copyright © 1979, 1980, 1982, Thomas Nelson, Inc., Publishers. Those marked NIV are from the Holy Bible, New International Version, copyright © 1973, 1978, 1984 by International Bible Society; and TLB, The Living Bible, copyright © Tyndale House Publishers, Wheaton, Ill., 1971, used by permission. Scripture quotations are from the ESV® Bible (The Holy Bible, English Standard Version®), copyright © 2001 by Crossway, a publishing ministry of Good News Publishers. Used by permission. All rights reserved.

ISBN-13: 978-1505205374
ISBN-10: 1505205379

1. *Southern Baptist Convention—Membership.*
2. *Revivals—United States—History—20th century.*
3. *Baptists—United States—Membership.*
4. *Evangelistic work— United States.*

I. *Avant, John, 1960- . Reid, Alvin, 1959- .*

CONTENTS

FOREWORD

HENRY BLACKABY

"Revival and spiritual awakening!" This has been the heart cry of multitudes for decades. God has been listening to our cry! In recent years, we have seen a marked increase in personal and corporate praying. But more significantly, we have seen a different kind of prayer. It is much more demanding.

As individuals, families, churches, denominations, and a nation, God has allowed us to have the opportunity to come to the point of desperation. Not all have taken the opportunity. Some have remained untouched and unmoved by the spiritual crisis in our lives, homes, communities, and nation. Others, however, have seen these times as a divine invitation to experience the heart of God and to "stand in the gap before [God] on behalf of the land" (Ezek. 22:30-31) in grave intercession, lest He bring rightful judgment upon our land.

Now more than ever, I have become aware of a growing number of spiritual leaders and the people of God "feeling the heart of God." When God is "ready to bring revival," He causes His people to come before Him in prayer. They instinctively:

* Pray—come to know the heart of God believe Him
* Repent (adjust their lives fully to Him)
* Obey Him

Then He moves among His people in mighty revival! And the world comes face to face with God and His salvation.

Not everyone wants revival. In the head, many want

revival; but in the heart, most do not. Jesus said, "'By their fruits you will know them'" (Matt. 7:20). When asked about revival, their affirmations are strong. When given the freedom to speak or plan, revival is rarely mentioned, if at all. However, the desperate cannot help but speak what is so heavy on their hearts and on the heart of God!

We are now seeing an "open cry of desperation"—an open and unashamed crying in great repentance, even brokenness, before the Lord. Real, life-changing repentance is becoming the common thread of experience in increasing numbers of student groups, churches, and meetings of Gods people, especially leaders. Jesus said, "'blessed are the pure in heart, for they shall see God'" (Matt. 5:8). The prayers of the righteous are powerful with God (see James 5:16-18), and the redeemed shall pass over the "Highway of Holiness" (Isa. 35:8). The prophet said, "The unclean shall not pass over it; but it shall be for others."

This is what we are seeing and experiencing—a deep sense of the presence of God, the holiness of God, the awesomeness of God, the true condition of our sin. We are seeing deep, honest repentance, followed by real, personal corporate "cleansing" by our Holy God. Like David, the cleansed can "teach transgressors Your ways, and sinners shall be converted to You" (Ps. 51:13). Revival by God's people always results in spiritual awakening in the hearts and lives of lost people.

We have joyfully been watching and participating in changing lives in ever-widening circles across the nation. I believe we are experiencing a "decade of harvest" as people around the world are coming to a saving experience of God's salvation in Jesus Christ in ever-increasing numbers.

May God grant us, in our day, eyes to see, and ears to hear, and hearts to understand (see Matt. 13:16-17). I believe God has in place those who will. It is a choice! We can:

* Come to Him
* Hear Him
* Obey Him (see Luke 6:46-49)

This book comes from hearts "that burn within," for they have encountered the Living Christ in His resurrection presence and power and purpose to save. This book is written with the prayer that an ever-widening circle of believers, who have been moved by God to pray for revival with increasing heart-intensity and faithfulness, will be greatly encouraged to respond to God in what Paul said: "And pray in the Spirit on all occasions with all kinds of prayers and requests. . .be alert and always keep on praying for all the saints" (Eph. 6:18, NIV). It is my prayer that we will, indeed, experience revival and great spiritual awakening in our day—for His name's sake!

ACKNOWLEDGEMENTS

Twenty years seem like a long time, and yet, in some ways it seems like yesterday.

We would like to thank those who have played a vital role in the preparation of this book. First, thanks to our sovereign Lord, the author of revival. The Lord has done great things for us, and we are glad!

John Landers of Broadman & Holman was tireless in his enthusiasm, faithful in his support, and patient with our questions in publication of the original version. To the contributors (listed at the end): you have been faithful on this project, and we thank you. Malcolm McDow served as an editor to the original edition, and we thank Malcolm for all he taught us. A special thanks to faithful secretaries, Becky Greer, Denise Koontz, and Bobby Harris for their assistance. Peggy Loafman helped immensely with the revised editing. Kevin Stone, Alvin's intern at his church, set the book up for publication. Thanks to others who proofread and otherwise assisted in this book.

Finally, we want to thank our precious families: our wives, Donna Avant, and Michelle Reid, and our children, Christi, Amy, and Trey; Joshua and Hannah Reid. Since the original edition was released they have all grown up and married. They were so long-suffering in our time away in the cause of revival, while burning the midnight oil at the computer, or while spending what seemed like half the day on the phone. You are the greatest!

REVIVAL REVIVED PREFACE TO THE REVISED EDITION

JOHN AVANT AND ALVIN L. REID

John Avant

20 years ago God wrecked my church and ruined my plans. And it was the greatest thing that has ever happened in my ministry! When God broke loose at Coggin Avenue Baptist Church on a normal Sunday in January of 1995, nothing would ever be the same in our church or in my life. God shelved all my own plans for the church where I was pastor and implemented His. He wrecked all our traditions and preferences and replaced them with His power and His glory.

Reading back through this material in preparation for this new edition of *Revival* brought a flood of memories and emotion. I found myself thinking, "All that actually happened! We got to see with our eyes and experience in our lives a great movement of God."

But I also found myself longing for *Revival Revived*—for a new season of revival today that would flood the earth with the glory of God, the Church with the power of God, and the nations with the message of God. I spoke with one of the students from the revival at Howard Payne University a few years ago and asked how the revival affects her today. She said, "I just can't be satisfied with 'business-as-usual' church anymore."

I get that! And we can't really afford business-as-usual anymore since the "usual" in the church is decline and division and the "usual" in the world is desperation and depravity.

But as we write this new edition, don't think that we long for God to do again what He did in 1995. We don't want that nor do we pray for that. This is not 1995. It is 2015. (Wow does that make me feel old!) We are not praying, "God do *it* again." We are praying for God to do something even more, something even greater; something unique to our day and to God's heart for the world of our day.

But we can learn much from the past. Those of us who were blessed to be a part of this revival movement had learned from awakenings of the past much that helped us to know how to respond and how to lead as God moved. We hope this book will play that same role for those who want to be prepared for the next time, prayerfully a time soon to come, where God moves in revival again.

In this book we have retained the accounts of revival from the various writers with very little editing. We hope that you will read these sections as more than history. Read them as the picture of the power of the living God moving mysteriously and wonderfully among His people. Read them as the preparation of God for pastors, missionaries and leaders in every walk of life who are now literally spread out across the face of the earth joining the Father in the advance of His kingdom.

To help you see how this has happened and the long-term impact of this movement, we have added a chapter called *Where Are They 20 Years Later* that allows you to see what God is doing now in the lives of many of those who were affected by the revival. We also have reflected on what we have learned ourselves through being a part of this movement in 2 chapters called *What We have Learned Through Revival.*

I conclude with a chapter entitled *A Ridiculous and Reasonable Hope* in which I discuss a hope for revival in our day, and a prayerful hypothesis of what it might look like if God moves and brings awakening again in this time and culture.

We have seen revival many times since 1995. I saw it in Southeast Asia when underground churches from all over a country gathered in secret. They wept over the chance to have the Lords Supper together. They crowded into small rooms with no air conditioning in 100-degree weather for hours. They sang all night. They left to take the gospel to their nation or die trying.

I saw it in the Middle East where I helped a former radical Muslim baptize a large number of new believers in an open courtyard in a neighborhood dominated by a terrorist group! More than 100 converted Muslims, the only church of Muslim background believers in that country, sang and praised as we baptized. Two terrorists witnessed the baptisms and came to us and prayed to receive Jesus on the spot! They insisted on being baptized too though they knew that their neighbors watching might kill them. When we baptized them, the church broke out in dance. They danced with joy for two hours—a Jesus party!

Revival is happening in many places around the world right now—in China, Africa, and Central America. But not here. Not in America. Stop right now and consider that. How does that make you feel? Do we really want to live our whole lives and never again see the power of God in this country? Does anything at all in our lives and our churches matter *more* than seeing God move in power again?

Then join us on a journey in this book into the past of 20 years ago and into the present intense prayer of our hearts for a great work of God that is the only hope to change our future. We have been blessed to see revival. Now we are ready for revival revived.

Alvin L. Reid

As a boy I saw God move in what we now call the Jesus Movement. I met Jesus in 1970 in what I learned later was the fastest growing small church in the Southern Baptist Convention, a church I also learned that was in the great minority of churches who let the hippies come into their services back then. I have never recovered from those days.

I met John Avant in seminary while preparing for the Ph.D. We were two of the earliest grads in the Ph.D. program at Southwestern Baptist Seminary in the evangelism track. Our hearts knit together with others in those days; we were galvanized together with a heart for revival.

We talked about revival, studied it academically, and prayed for it together. We just were not quite ready when it came in 1995! The good news is that God is still at work. I've seen signs of the activity of God often since then. I saw it in a church in South Carolina where services went for hours and the number of people saved stretched across the entire front of the church. I've seen it in a remarkable young lady named Alisa who was transformed by the gospel in Chiang Mai, Thailand, on the first international missions trip with my daughter. I've seen it in a student named J.D. who started a Bible study that exploded on his college campus and now leads one of the most dynamic churches in America where huge numbers of collegians and young professionals come to faith annually. I've seen it in reports of friends coming from the depths of the persecuted church where believers who have nothing only want to live for Jesus and never complain about their circumstance. How we pray for that spirit in the American church!

But the American church needs a fresh touch from God. This week I will baptize two new believers in their 20s at our church. That is more than 80% of churches in my tradition, the Southern Baptist Convention, will reach in an entire year. You will read the stories in these pages of many 20something year olds who were ablaze for God. Perhaps the reason the church today struggles with reaching young adults has something to do with the lack of passion for God they see in us. The sad reality is that most young adults in our churches, including most of my students, have never seen a movement of revival. When we talk about it in class they hunger for it. G. Campbell Morgan said that a sailor has no effect on the wind, but a good sailor knows well how to set the sails when the wind blows. We pray that these accounts of revival and the things we have learned will help you to know better when the Spirit begins to blow, and will help you to set the sails to join His movement!

PART ONE
IGNITION

The following pages recount the work of God leading up to and beginning in Brownwood, Texas, at Coggin Avenue Baptist Church, neighboring churches, and Howard Payne University. We pray these eyewitness accounts will come alive as you read them that you will experience the fresh fire of God these testimonies describe.

Lord,
We call out to You for genuine awakening on Howard
Payne's
campus that could send out literally hundreds and
hundreds of
students to every corner of this nation and world with a
fire of
revival in their hearts.

CHAPTER 1
PREPARATION FOR REVIVAL

MALCOLM MCDOW AND ALVIN L. REID

The above prayer was offered by Pastor John Avant on Sunday night, January 29. A few weeks later, students from Howard Payne University did go out, if not in hundreds, at least in ones, twos, fours, and fives, to spread the news of a true movement of God on their campus. Two people who were particularly used in the revival are Henry Blackaby and John Avant.

HENRY BLACKABY AND *EXPERIENCING GOD*

Blackaby, former director of the Office of Prayer and Spiritual Awakenings for the Home Mission Board (SBC, now the North American Mission Board), has had a passion for revival and awakening since he was a lad in his native Canada. Hear his story:

> My heritage goes back to England, where several of my family were graduates of Spurgeon's College at a time when Spurgeon was trying to

win England to Christ. I grew up in a town in Canada where there was no evangelical witness to Christ. My father served as a lay pastor to help start a mission in that town. In my teen years I began to sense a deep burden for communities across Canada that did not have an evangelical church. In 1958 when I was in seminary, God assured me that He loved my nation enough to want to bring a great movement of His Spirit across our land. When I accepted the call to go to Saskatoon as a pastor, God used the prospect of a spiritual awakening there to affirm my call—a spiritual awakening that started there spread all across Canada in the early 1970s.

From 1988 until only recently Blackaby worked with leaders from across denominational lines to call churches in America to return to God and cry out for revival.

Blackaby's greatest impact came through *Experiencing God* and *Fresh Encounter,* small-group discipleship manuals he published with Claude King. *Experiencing God* swept the nation and spread to many denominations. More than a million copies have been sold and have led countless individuals to personal renewal and churches to encounter God in fresh ways. Many churches and students in the 1995 revival used *Experiencing God.* A trade book by the same name was one of the top twenty-five evangelical books as selected by *Christianity Today* in 1995. The manual guides people to understand how God involves people in His work:

1. God is always at work around you.

2. God pursues a continuing love relationship with you that is real and personal.

3. God invites you to become involved with Him in His work.

4. God speaks by the Holy Spirit through the Bible, prayer, circumstances, and the church to reveal Himself, His purposes, and His ways.

5. God's invitation for you to work with Him always leads you to a crisis of belief that requires faith and action.

6. You must make major adjustments in your life to join God in what He is doing.

7. You come to know God by experience as you obey Him and He accomplishes His work through you.

A second workbook entitled *Fresh Encounter* focused even more on the specific subject of revival and spiritual awakening.

JOHN AVANT

The other key person is John Avant, pastor at the time of the Coggin Avenue Baptist Church. What occurred in January 1995 did not come out of a vacuum. The following is Avant's narrative of events preceding the revival:

In the 1980's Roy Fish introduced me to the term *spiritual awakening* in a course by that name at Southwestern Baptist Seminary.

I will never forget a day in a Ph.D. seminar on spiritual awakening when a student spoke up and asked, "Why have we never heard of these things? Why has nobody in our churches heard of these things? Why have deacons never heard of the Great Awakenings?" After the moral failure by a leading Dallas pastor, one student in the seminar said, "If we fail like this, we will never see a mighty awakening, and another generation will have forgotten what God has done in history." We began to weep, and God poured out His Spirit upon us that day.

Out of that seminar came an accountability group. Five men from that seminar—Steve Gaines, Doug Munton, Alvin Reid, Preston Nix, and I—determined to meet at the Southern Baptist Convention every year. Our wives and we pray as long as God leads us. Our prayer has been, "Lord, kill us before we would ever shame your name." And our other prayer has been, "Lord, please let revival come!"

BROKENNESS

As my ministry began to take on the appearance of success my heart departed radically from the Father. The thing that frightens me the most is that I never recognized how far I had departed into pride, which is my besetting sin. I figured that when you get a Ph.D. in evangelism and when you are pastor of a growing church, you should move on to that mega church. So I put out my resumes and pulled strings. One day, the mega church came calling. I was about to head there as the pastor when, at the last possible moment, one of the members of that committee changed his mind. My life was devastated, and I was angry with God.

I prayed, "OK, God, I will stay here if You wish." But I was bitter toward God. Then in 1992, in the midst of preaching in Indianapolis, I became ill. I was sick for three months. I got so sick that I could hardly continue my ministry. The only thing the doctors could tell me was that I had some viral condition and that they could not find a cure.

I went to a summer Bible conference and shared with Henry Blackaby and Roy Fish. As I studied Scripture, I recommitted myself to the Lord. God assured my heart that He would take me out of the pit, but not until I was willing to be obedient to Him instead of to my own plans.

A church in Brownwood, Texas, had telephoned me before God began to change my heart, but I had no interest at that time. Where in the world is Brownwood? It is an hour and a half from anything in any direction. I knew only suburban areas or big cities had mega churches. I refused to submit my resume there, yet somebody sent it without my knowledge. When the committee called, I had no interest whatsoever. My wife, Donna, even scolded me for being rude to a committee member on the phone.

But after my personal revival that summer, God began to turn my heart and I sensed Him saying, "You must be obedient to Me and go where I tell you to go." But I said, "But, God, I am sick." And He said, "I didn't ask you if you were sick." The illness did not begin to go away until I was actually on the church field. In fact, I thought I would pass out preaching my trial sermon.

PREPARATION AT BROWNWOOD

Brownwood is the hub of west central Texas. Howard Payne University is there, a Texas Baptist university with about fourteen hundred students. But the city and the church faced serious spiritual challenges. There were some wonderful people but also some serious problems in the church. Many of the things I tried were opposed.

One day I reached my breaking point. I sat with the

chairman of the pulpit committee in his pickup truck and cried. I said, "I don't know why God brought me here. I can't do anything with these people." Just then, God broke my heart and reminded me what He tried to teach me in my sickness. No, I could not do anything with those people. Only God could do anything with His people.

THE FIRE IGNITES

Gradually, there began to be a turning. It was not immediate; in fact, there were many barriers along the way. Slowly we began to see a hunger and a growing sense of expectancy. People began to sign up for classes to study the *Experiencing God* materials. Pretty soon three hundred people in our church had been through *Experiencing God.* Our people began to thirst a little more. Our church canceled our regular evening services and went through *Fresh Encounter.* Still there was no genuine revival.

Then God began doing unusual things. He began showing His power to the people of our church and our community in ways I would have never dreamed!

God began to do a great work in the lives of some of our men. One man named J. R., who had been deeply touched by the Lord, began to share with others.

One day J. R. went to a car dealership to talk with another well-known man in the community named Rick. Rick was only days away from seeing his divorce become final. When J. R. came in, Rick said, "I can't believe you are here. I was hoping somebody would come that I could talk to." J. R. said, "Can we go talk with the pastor?" The three of us had lunch together. I said, "Rick, why don't you bring Jennifer, and let's talk."

Rick and Jennifer came into my office and poured out their hearts—a painful story of a family on the verge of destruction. I thought, *there is no hope here apart from Jesus.* As I shared with them, they came to the point of saying, "We have got to have Jesus. He is our only hope." I did something that I have never done before—I did not lead them to Jesus. Instead, I picked up the phone and called J. R. He had never led anybody to Christ before. I sent them to J. R., who led them to the Lord and brought them down the aisle the next Sunday with weeping and tears. The eyes of our people became as large as saucers as they began to see the power of God.

Rick went home and said, "Boys, come here, I have something to tell you." One son ran to his room crying. He thought his daddy had come to say the divorce was final and he was never coming back. Rick went to him and said, "Son, come here." The boy replied, "No, Daddy, I can't. Daddy, I have prayed twice a day to Jesus that He would bring you back home, and I don't want to hear about divorce." And Rick said, "Bryce, you don't understand. Jesus has come into my life, and I have come home!" That little boy fell into the arms of his daddy. He had a family again! Today that family is in church every time the doors are open. They have been radically transformed by the power of God. People began to watch and wonder, if *just maybe God could do something through His power that we could never do ourselves.*

FERNANDO HERNANDEZ—AN UNLIKELY MESSENGER

One day someone brought Fernando to see me. We

were still far from revival. A church member said, "I want you to meet Fernando. He has a ministry."

Fernando was a former drug addict, had been in jail, and had done nearly everything that a person could do. On one occasion he overdosed and almost died. On another, his wife told him, "Fernando, look in the mirror. What you see is not a man because a man takes care of his wife and children." Through the love of his mother and his wife, he accepted Jesus. God completely changed his life, and he came to Brownwood.

After his conversion, Fernando became convinced God had a plan and purpose for him. When he came to Brownwood, he became a dishwasher at a restaurant. One day I went into the restaurant and I left a little witnessing card on the table. The waiter took it back to Fernando. He saw it and said, "God, maybe this is the person that I need to talk to." So, he stuck the card on a mirror over where he washed dishes. He never told me this until after our church was officially supporting his ministry.

God laid it upon my heart that we were to support him as a church. I brought the issue to our church and said, "Folks, I just want you to see something." Fernando paraded in some gang kids with whom he had been working. Brownwood had a Hispanic gang problem, but these kids had been completely changed by the power of God after being helped by Fernando. The young men trembled with fear standing before the large congregation. They shared simple testimonies like, "I was a drug addict, living on the street, and Jesus changed my life." Seeing lives so changed by the gospel made quite an impact. Our church unanimously voted to join in this mission effort—a joint project between a Baptist church and a charismatic church! God began to work. Pretty soon we started baptizing kids from the gangs. In the fall of 1995, we had baptized thirty kids from his ministry. Only one parent ever came to watch the baptism.

One day the junior high principal contacted Fernando, who has about an eighth-grade education and no GED. He said, "Fernando, I have so many problems! Would you come and talk to our kids?" Fernando said, "The only thing I know to tell them is Jesus." The principal replied, "If that will help, then go ahead."

The principal brought the whole school into the auditorium for an assembly, and turned it over to a man who had been in jail and who could hardly read. Fernando said, "Let me just tell you about my life, and let me tell you what changed it." He told them about Jesus. Later the principal said, "I am going to set up an office for you here. You can do anything you want. Before school, after school, or during school, whatever you want."

The high school principal called and said, "Listen, will you come and have an office at the high school too, and be a counselor at our high school?" Fernando never attended high school! God has taken this unbelievably desperate life and changed it forever!

UNITY IN THE FAITH

We began to witness God's mighty power when the charismatic church found out that we didn't hate them, and we discovered that they didn't hate us. We started having a prayer group together. Soon it included Nazarene, Methodist, Baptist, Pentecostal, Church of Christ, and Assembly of God's pastors. We started to pray, "God, we don't care about our differences. We just want to see Jesus bring revival into this community."

God began to unify our churches, and *Experiencing God* began to sweep across denominational lines. People who had nothing to do with Baptist life began going through *Experiencing God.* Once the charismatic pastor said, "John, you must know this. We have many people going through *Experiencing God* at our church, and it has changed our lives. We have a group right now that is led by a Presbyterian, meeting in a charismatic church full of charismatics, with a Church of Christ pastor in it, and it is Baptist material. It has *got* to be revival!"

IN GOD'S OWN TIME

I thought God would do something in our church right after our people went through *Experiencing God,* but it didn't happen then. God was preparing us for what was to come. The training helped prepare our people to be more available and open. *Experiencing God* probably kept our folks from having coronaries at the thought of three-hour services and ninety-minute invitations when revival came!

Our students began to develop a hunger and thirst to see the Lord in a new way. One former Howard Payne student named Jason had prayed for revival for years, but he left college feeling that his prayers were unanswered.

He saw a lot of apathy and sin. He shared his broken heart with many before he left. But when revival came, Jason took time off from where he was serving as youth pastor of a church in west Texas, came back to the campus, sat on the front row worshiping God, saying, "Thank You, Jesus. You did answer my prayers."

We prayed, believed, and hoped that God might bring revival. Many of us sensed when we saw these things happening that God was doing something that we could not do ourselves. There was a growing sense of expectancy. We looked forward to February 1995 when Henry Blackaby was coming to town for the annual revival services at Howard Payne University. That seemed to be the perfect time, but God had other plans.

In 1992, I was on a Home Mission Board tour of our mission work in New England. I visited Yale University, where once a great revival came in the spring of 1802. I had studied how the president, Timothy Dwight, led in the awakening. God brought this sweeping revival as a part of the Second Great Awakening. However, Yale had become spiritually dead; there was very little life on that campus anymore.

During a meeting I whispered to my wife, "I want to go see if the place where Timothy Dwight preached is still standing." It is still there—a little old building between two big new buildings. I wanted to go in and see what it must have been like once upon a time when there was an awakening in this country.

As I opened a big door, I thought I was hearing things—there was a student singing the chorus "Alleluia, Alleluia." At first the light was so dim that I could hardly see. Then I saw a young Korean man on his knees before the lectern singing to the Lord. As the doors closed behind me, he was startled. We began to weep. I told him who I was and why I was there. He then shared with me how he had been saved in Korea, had come to America, and had studied about the revivals of our nation. He couldn't understand why there were so few believers on campus. He said to me, "Everyday I come here, and I kneel before the place where Timothy Dwight preached, and I pray that once again God will bring revival to America." I agreed to join him in that prayer.

I don't know what God wants to do with what is happening in our city, but could it be that God might be answering the prayers of that young Korean believer? In Acts 4:31 it says, "When they had prayed, the place where they were assembled together was shaken; and they were all filled with the Holy Spirit, and they spoke the Word of God with boldness." We need to pray. Maybe God will come upon us again.

CHAPTER 2
REVIVAL AT
BROWNWOOD

SELECTIONS FROM THE JOURNAL OF JOHN AVANT

Wednesday, January 25, 1995. This is the account of what the Lord began at Coggin Avenue Baptist Church on Sunday morning, January 22. It was Sanctity of Life Sunday, and the Lord showered His life-giving Spirit upon us. I began a sermon series on the Ten Commandments with the first command, "'You shall have no other gods before me'"(Exod. 20:3).

LET GOD BE GOD

Our early service began as normal, about 8:30 A.M. with the auditorium about half full. But there was something a little different. Usually few, if any, students attend the early service, but this Sunday there were about thirty university students present. When I offered the invitation, Chris Robeson, a student leader on campus, came forward and asked if he could speak. Ordinarily, I would have told him to talk to me after the service, but God led me to allow him to speak.

Chris stood at the pulpit and read Joel 2:12: "Turn to Me with all your heart, with fasting, with weeping, and with mourning." He began to weep and cry out to the Lord. He shared his desperate burden that the time had come for revival. People began to stream down the aisles. A woman in our church challenged our people that we were not a praying church and that we needed to begin to pray and seek God diligently. She asked, "If we don't turn back to Him in prayer, what is God going to do with us?" People started coming to the microphone spontaneously, sharing Scripture and sharing their hearts. The altar was full of people on their knees and on their faces.

By now it was time for Sunday school, but it was obvious that the Lord was dealing with us in a deep way. I told the people that they could stay, go to their classes and tell others to come to the services, or go to their classes for the Sunday school hour—whatever they wanted to do. Most of the people stayed.

A dear lady named Nita, who had been in the early service, was sitting at the table outside the Sunday school office crying. When the people came by looking for their class and could find no one, they went to her and asked, "What is wrong? Has somebody died? What has happened?" Nita simply pointed to the sanctuary. People continually came in and joined those still gathered.

Someone went to our Christian Life Center and told our university students, "God has come to the sanctuary!" and they came into the sanctuary. Many students said later that, as soon as they opened the door to enter, they sensed God's power and presence.

We continued with praise, prayer, sharing, and singing all through the Sunday school hour. People were coming to the altar broken for sin. Tim Ward, another of our students, shared Habakkuk 2:1-4, verses the Lord had specifically led him to share. He didn't know it, but these had become the theme verses for our church's vision statement. We had voted on the statement the week before when the students were on Christmas break. I had preached on this very passage, but he had no idea.

People began to come in for the 11:00 service. They didn't know what was going on, but they joined in with us in seeking God. Many of them came spontaneously to kneel at the altar. We were live on the radio at 11:00, but our entire structure for the service had changed. As we were going on the air, we were in the midst of an invitation. People were still streaming down the aisles. It was obvious they were ready to respond. Twenty-two people were saved or called to the ministry during that invitation.

In response to what God was doing among us, I said, "Please don't go out of here and say, 'We had revival and it was great!' When you go out of here, say, 'We are *having* revival, and it is great!' Revival is not one event. It is wonderful and magnificent—the power and presence of the Spirit of God. But it is the *beginning* of something, that is all."

A woman came up and said, "I have to leave after Sunday school and go play the piano at another church. Would you pray for me and for that church?" We stopped what we were doing and prayed for her. We prayed for revival to break out in that church and in other churches.

Later that day we found out that the Rocky Creek Baptist Church broke out in revival at the very same time, even though they were unaware of what was happening in our church. Pastor Mark Bryant challenged the members there to "live outside the lines." At that point people spontaneously flooded the altar, praying and seeking God in brokenness and repentance. We also found out that First Baptist, Santa Anna, a small community close to Brownwood, had twenty-one saved in the morning service and twenty-seven other commitments that day—forty-eight in all. They said this was the greatest harvest of people coming to know Jesus they had ever seen. Trinity Chapel, another church in our area, also broke out in revival on January 22. The pastor, Dan Chapman, is beside himself with joy! The pastor at the Assembly of God Church stopped preaching in the middle of his message and sensed God wanted to bring revival to our churches that very day. He called this whole church to the altar to pray. All this on the same day.

REVIVAL! WHAT NOW?

I went home that afternoon scared to death. I had prayed for revival. Now it had come and I wasn't sure we were ready! How would the people respond? I said to my wife, "Donna, we prayed for this, so why am I so scared?" I realized that, in a fairly traditional Baptist church, I had virtually canceled Sunday school. I said, "I may be serving as pastor of a new church next week. They may run me off!" All afternoon I wondered how the people would respond, especially the senior adults.

That night we had a joint service scheduled with our Hispanic mission. The group had already begun to experience something of a revival themselves, with a new pastor and new growth, when it looked like the mission might fold. That night our auditorium was packed with whites, blacks, and Hispanics. God just fell on that service. The Brownwood community struggles with racial problems, but suddenly the altar filled with all three racial groups crying out to God. We baptized sixteen troubled young people from Fernando Hernandez's ministry. The power of God was evident in the service. Two more people have come to Christ since

Sunday because of the sharing of revived people, and we have seven more awaiting baptism.

That night at a fellowship after the service people began to share their response to the revival. I couldn't believe the support. Our senior adults were simply wonderful! No complaint, no opposition. They came to me one by one, saying, "Oh, Pastor, thank you for not hindering what God did." One of our senior adults told me he had prayed for forty years that God would let him live to see revival in his church. Now God was answering his prayer. Another senior adult expressed willingness to share his testimony and his excitement about what God is doing.

I've now been told about other churches outside of our area that had tremendous revival-type services on January 22. One of our members who was at Fielder Road Baptist Church in Arlington, Texas, said it was an absolutely incredible service.

Tim Navratil, one of our church leaders, and his wife missed the service because they were in a weekend *Experiencing God* marriage retreat. They had a revival experience that has changed their lives. They sought God together and asked God to bring revival to our church. They prayed that on Saturday, January 21. We since found out that Alamo City Baptist Church in San Antonio began on Saturday, January 21, a week of prayer and fasting, calling the entire church to pray for revival.

FROM COGGIN TO HOWARD PAYNE

Thursday, January 26. Could what has happened in our service be spreading to the Howard Payne University campus? Howard Payne is a Baptist school with about fourteen hundred students led by president Don

Newbury, a wonderful, strong Christian leader. There are some fine Christian administrators there, including Bill Fishback, and faculty who are leaders in our church. It seems that perhaps God is beginning to move in revival on the campus.

Some students had begun to develop a hunger and thirst to see the Lord move in a fresh way. They were convinced God was going to do something special. We've been told of students stopping on campus in groups of twos and threes, and simply praying together wherever they stand. One young man told me that today, as he walked across campus, everywhere he went he encountered students praying and seeking God. There will be a special service held on campus tomorrow night to seek God for revival.

AND THE PEOPLE PRAYED

Friday, January 27. The service on campus was a marvelous experience, and students are indeed opening their hearts to revival. There are now prayer meetings occurring in the rooms of students, some before class in the morning, some late at night. Relationships are being restored in the lives of many of the students in remarkable ways. We've also heard about another church in Fort Worth that entered revival on Sunday. Our Coggin Avenue women are beginning spontaneous prayer groups in their homes.

Thursday, February 2. So much is beginning to happen now I cannot journal every day. I am going to have to journal every few days and summarize what is happening. Revival continues. On Sunday, January 29, two of our senior adults shared their testimonies in both our early and late morning worship services about what

God was doing in their hearts in revival. The man who had prayed for forty years that God would send revival shared. People were overwhelmed. Wonderful testimonies, wonderful stories! I preached on getting rid of idols and laying down sin. There was a deep response at the altar. More people came to know Jesus.

When I planned my preaching program last year, I scheduled to preach on praying for revival on the evening of January 29. I didn't realize that was Super Bowl Sunday. I felt led to keep that schedule. I was so proud of our men, to see so many of them come to church that night and pray for revival and read what the Word of God says about praying for revival. We had another moving of the Spirit of God that evening.

We now have another home prayer meeting group made up of people from our church. I have heard reports of many prayer groups on campus. Other churches are entering into revival. The pastor of Southside Assembly of God told me that, on January 22, they felt led of God to have a special prayer time for revival for other churches in the community on that day. At the Ministerial Alliance this week, we had thirty minutes of sharing about what God was doing. The chaplain at the Havins Unit, a Texas Department of Corrections drug treatment center, told us he had recently baptized sixteen and had twenty-five more wanting to know Jesus. He wants about fifty of our men to come, share, disciple, and conduct a revival meeting.

A woman wrote a letter to me dated January 14. I had not had time to read it thoroughly until recently. She said she is not a church member but believes God is going to do something great in Brownwood; she even says that some of her friends were moving here to be a part of what God is going to do.

Ron Owens called me from Atlanta and asked me to go to Convocation on Revival in Little Rock after Henry Blackaby is here with us. The Intercessory Prayer Line at the Home Mission Board now has a request for the campus at Howard Payne. It says that the university is experiencing a move from God that is similar to the Asbury movement in 1970, and that this may be the breakthrough for which we have prayed. I had previously told Henry Blackaby what had been happening in our church.

On a Wednesday night, I met with students, called the prayer line, and let the students hear the message. They began to cry and hug each other. One girl told me, "Brother John, I feel like the people must have felt when they heard Neil Armstrong talk from the moon for the first time. To think that people all over the nation are praying for our school!" They called parents and others saying, "God is coming to our school. Pray for our campus!"

A pastor from Germantown Baptist Church in Washington, D.C., called that prayer line. Then he called Howard Payne, and someone referred him to us. He said his church had been led to pray for spiritual awakening for three years and would be praying for us. Word of what God is doing seems to be spreading like wildfire. Students' hearts are more open than I have ever seen.

LIVING OUTSIDE THE LINES

The Wednesday night prayer meeting was like a revival service. The Spirit moved in, and our people opened and shared their hearts. They prayed in large and small groups, pouring out their hearts for revival. One man shared with me that this revival had so changed his life that he is now praying for one hour every morning starting at 5:00 A.M. This revival has transformed his whole life and his marriage!

We are also beginning to hear of things happening related to our January 22 service. In Pioneer, Texas, a rancher who was a strong believer had to go take care of a cow that was giving birth to a calf that morning and could not go to church. He had with him a fifty-year-old ranch hand. Due to the cold, they sat in the truck and listened to our service over the radio. The ranch hand was so moved that he asked how to receive Jesus. The rancher told him, and he received Jesus that day. He asked what to do next, and he was told to be baptized. They couldn't find a church in that little area with a baptistry, so they found a pastor who later baptized him outside on that cold day.

Monday, February 6. Yesterday we began with a "dry" early service. I told the people it seemed there were barriers in their hearts. Some prayed through Sunday school because of the "dryness" in that service. Some prayed at the altar, some in the prayer room, some in the balcony. Then the Spirit again fell on the 11:00 service. Tim Navratil shared a powerful testimony. I shared about how the ranch hand had been saved in Pioneer and about the Home Mission Board prayer line. Families began to come forward to be restored with each other. Two more came to profess Jesus. The altar again was full, and the power of God was visibly evident. The service went on for a long time.

Sunday night was incredible. We baptized five. The young people were in charge of the entire service to share what God had done in their lives. They had a special weekend called Heartbeat Weekend where they had a *Disciple Now* emphasis that included staying in the homes of church members. Some of our adults shared what God had done in their lives as they had seen the youth praying for revival.

A Taiwanese student came forward. Revived members of our church had led him to Christ. When asked to fill out the information card used during the invitation, he didn't know how. He started writing his testimony on the back: "I was reared a Buddhist. My family is Buddhist. But I have come to know Jesus. He is my only hope and my only Savior, and I will serve Him all my life." The people applauded and cried out in praise to the Lord. The altar again was flooded.

As others came and shared, there was much weeping. The service was long, but no one left. One man commented, "What are we going to do—go home and watch television?" The service began at six and lasted until nine.

Tuesday, February 7. I just found out that Richard, the Taiwanese student who was saved, was a man whom Bill Fishback, a member and administrator at Howard Payne, had asked prayer for on a Wednesday night service. Now eight more Taiwanese students are open to the gospel. We also know that four Howard Payne football players have experienced a powerful revival. Some of them shared at that Sunday night service. There are tastes of revival on the Howard Payne athletic teams.

Wednesday, February 8. I received a call tonight from Matt Dowling. He was so excited he could hardly speak. He said thirteen guys experienced an incredible revival in a dorm room at Howard Payne tonight. They began with prayer. There was deep confession of sin. They found out that they were struggling with some of the same sins, and God's power fell on them.

We are also hearing of something the students call "Jesus parties." They get together and spend hours at a time in worship and praise. Sometimes they go all night long. We just received a letter from a junior high student. Three more junior high students have been led to Christ by our students and will make their professions of faith Sunday morning. In the letter she said she is so excited she can hardly write. She says all anyone can talk about at lunch is Jesus.

Students are now coming to them and asking how to be saved because of the strong move of God in our junior high. She says, *"God is rocking the nation, and it's all starting in Brownwood."* That's becoming something of a slogan for many of our young people.

CAMPUS RUMBLINGS

Thursday, February 9. The Howard Payne newspaper, *Yellow Jacket,* reads "Revival an Everyday Occurrence for Students." It is now clear that there is a strong revival movement on campus, not among all the students, but among a large number who are daily walking with God in revival. Another headline reads, "Students Reap Years of Harvest in Revival." The students write, "Is God preparing HPU for the spring revival with Henry Blackaby, or are God's plans for HPU greater than anyone of us could hope or dream?" One student is quoted as saying, "Over the next several weeks, God is going to 'bust' loose on this campus." The article also described the Jesus parties.

The students seem to be catching a vision for the possibility that God could use them in a far greater way because of the revival that He has brought to them. It's exciting to see their vision, that they are recognizing that God can really use them.

I had prayer with President Don Newbury today. Praise God for such a godly leader on our campus. He is wide open to whatever God may want to do on campus. As Henry Blackaby comes for revival services, Dr. Newbury will allow the students even to be late to class or miss class, whatever God wants to do.

Today I talked with Richard, our Taiwanese student. He said he is so excited to know more about what he calls the "Christ life" as he grows as a believer.

UNITY IN CHRIST

We continue to hear of other churches and members who have experienced revival. We've been excited to see how *Experiencing God* has spread.

Monday, February 13. Henry Blackaby came to be with us on February 11. God used him in the most powerful way I have ever seen. Yesterday morning I walked into the church office to get ready for the early service. Tim Holder, our minister of music, walked into the sanctuary and came out with tears in his eyes. He whispered, "God is in there!" And He was. That day we undoubtedly had the largest attendance in the history of our church— maybe twelve to thirteen hundred people packed into our services. The power of God came. People were responding with brokenness and repentance as Henry preached. Others were baptized. We are baptizing every Sunday. The service went well beyond our normal time as the invitation extended.

Sunday night twenty to thirty churches, some from out-of-town, canceled their services and came for the service that lasted more than three hours. At one point all the pastors and staff members came to the altar. There were so many we could not kneel. I said, "We need to pray for our churches." They began to cry out, "Oh, God, please change me." "Oh, Lord, forgive my wickedness." "Lord, heal my church." "Lord, forgive my sin." "Lord, forgive my evil heart." All kinds of deep prayers! Members from different churches jammed into the auditorium, crying and pouring out their hearts. As the people watched their pastors and staff members, they were overwhelmed. Then people began to come forward to pray for lost family members. Henry had preached on this. This was one of the greatest experiences in worship I have had in my entire life.

Henry had shared in Sunday school with our college students, preparing them for what God was going to do on campus. There was such expectancy it is hard to describe it. These students had been preparing themselves, praying, seeking God, worshiping in their dorm rooms. They are ready for God to do something in their lives.

CHAPTER 3
HOWARD PAYNE—A CAMPUS ABLAZE

CONTINUED FROM JOHN AVANT'S JOURNAL

TAKING OFF THE MASK

Tuesday, February 14. On Monday, God began to work in a powerful way on campus. As Henry shared in chapel, there was deep movement and deep response among the students. We are hearing that people are praying and fasting in our church and other churches. All over town and in other places, people are calling to tell us they are praying for us.

Wednesday, February 15. Yesterday was one of the greatest days that I have ever experienced in ministry. We had a noon luncheon after Henry Blackaby spoke in chapel.

About three hundred gathered from all over the community. Many were business people, but there were also several pastors. Henry shared; it was powerful. We stood for a closing prayer. As we tried to close, a man began to cry out. He confessed his sin of pornography. A missionary from Uganda began to weep and cry out for revival. As we held hands to close, people all across the room began to call out in repentance and open confession of sin. Spontaneously, they asked forgiveness for pride, greed, lust, and pornography. An hour later we were still holding hands. People finally left for work, overwhelmed by the Spirit of God.

I had been praying that God would break through and

lead our students to deal with sin. When two students came to me, I sensed from God that I was not to initiate anything, but I was to let Him do what He wanted. Jay Jones (name changed for security reasons) and Richard Robeson (Chris's brother), two leaders on our campus, said they felt the urging of God that they were to share with the students in the campus service that night. I introduced them to Henry and left them with him. At Henry's suggestion, they spent the rest of the afternoon in prayer.

That night we had a wonderful service—six or seven hundred students, maybe more were in attendance. The auditorium was full. At the end I still didn't know whether Henry would call on the students, but he did. Jay was first. He said, "You think that I have been such a good Christian, but I've been wearing a mask. Tonight I am taking off the mask." He just laid down on his face before the Lord on the platform. Richard shared about his own sin. The male students came and gathered around them.

Then a young lady came and shared how she and other ladies had not been helping the men. She said they were ashamed of the way they had been dressing. As I stood behind them, counseling a student, I heard what sounded like a stampede. I looked, and the ladies, a hundred or more, were on stage, weeping.

Dozens of people began coming to the microphone. There were 300-400 students at the altar! I never got an accurate count on how many shared confessions of sin, but it went on for three hours. By eleven o'clock, the students finished. One student had come in the midst of the service and accepted Christ. Another student began to laugh during his testimony. He said, "I'm so free!" He added, "Hold me accountable, for you will find that I have been set free.

As they finally finished, they gathered around the piano and sang praises to the Lord. When I left at 11:15, they were still singing praises. Some stayed up all night, seeking God in prayer in their dorms.

This morning's chapel was powerful. Henry preached about how Thomas had missed seeing Jesus, but God gave him another chance. Henry challenged the students who had missed the Tuesday night service to let the Lord do something in them and bring revival in their hearts. He read Isaiah 35. He preached about the Highway of Holiness. He said that God could use the students as a highway of holiness for revival to spread if they would walk with God (see chapter 6).

A father told how he had prayed over the campus. During the son's freshman year the father had said, "Son, I believe in my heart God will bring a spiritual awakening to this campus before you finish." His son is a senior and will graduate in May.

FROM BROWNWOOD TO LITTLE ROCK

Henry surprised me yesterday when he said he had conferred with the leaders in Little Rock, and they felt that he and I should share at the National Convocation on Revival. They had given us an unlimited time to share. I was fearful at the thought of getting in the way of God, or letting my pride get in the way, or of being unable to put it into words. But I began to prepare my heart. I shared my fears with my wife. Our eleven-year-old daughter, Christi, heard me talk about how frightened I was and wrote a letter. My wife saw the letter on my pillow and brought it to me, and we wept together. Christi had written:

> Dear Daddy,
>
> I just want to let you know that I will be praying for you until the time you speak. Daniel was afraid too and so was Joshua. In my quiet time book I am learning how to be courageous. Remember this verse, Daddy: "Be strong and very courageous. Be careful to obey all the laws my servant Moses gave you. Do not turn from it to the right or to the left so that you may be successful wherever you go. I will never leave you or forsake you" Joshua 1:5. Daddy, if God can use Daniel, He can use you. God is going to rock the nation, Daddy. Love, Christi

Knowing the prayers of so many and the prayers of my own children gave me peace.

NATIONAL CONVOCATION ON REVIVAL

Thursday, February 16. The Little Rock airport shut down, so we were unable to get to the Convocation in time for the service. My first reaction was disappointment at missing my chance to speak. God spoke to my heart and said if I never am able to share what God has done, simply what has happened in my life and in my church is enough. Yet today I discovered Henry and I will be speaking to close out the Convocation.

Friday, February 17. Henry and I shared last night. It was a tremendous experience. The people were so affirming. There was a hunger. After we shared, people filled the altar area. People came to the microphone and pleaded for prayer for their churches. They asked me to share, or to send students to share with their people. It was one of those moments when you sense that God is bringing His reviving work farther and deeper than we had ever dreamed.

WEIGHING ON GOD'S SCALES

Monday, February 20. I returned on Friday in time for our deacons' retreat. This was a breakthrough for our church. I had our men go through a revival prayer checklist that lines up their lives beside Jesus' teachings in the Sermon on the Mount. Each spent thirty to forty-five minutes alone on the campgrounds. When they returned, they were quiet. One deacon stood up and said something to the effect, "I'm not sure after doing this that I know God. I can't check any of these correctly." Men began to deal with and confess sin. There was a genuine sense of brokenness and revival among our deacons.

FELLOWSHIP RESTORED

Normally on Saturday night I walk through the sanctuary and pray for those who will be there the next day. As I left that night our maintenance man, a fairly new believer whose life had been touched by revival, continued to pray as he worked.

In the early service yesterday morning, there was a tremendous response. At the end of the service, a man and his wife came forward. I couldn't believe it, because he was a man with whom I had a broken relationship for a long time. Both of us had almost given up on any hope of restoring our relationship. I was so overwhelmed I could hardly speak. I wept before God. There we stood in reconciliation. He gave me permission to share what he and his wife had done. One of our deacons who was sick at home heard it on the radio, laid on his bed, and cried. Many people in the church knew about the relationship problem. It was an incredible healing and such a release. It led to other relationships being restored as well.

That night we opened the microphones and allowed people to confess sin. The service lasted a long time. We had to cut it off and agreed to pick it up again later. Some of the confessions were very deep.

One man shared that the last time he had been to the altar was when he was saved at the age of twelve. He was now recommitting his life to the Lord. As he knelt in prayer his wife joined him, and soon others joined him in prayer. That same man was part owner of a bar in town. We didn't know it. He has since shut down the bar.

Also yesterday we had a commitment time to be on mission with what God had done. Many adults and students committed to share their faith with everyone God gave them opportunity and to share the reviving work that God had brought to their lives.

A press release about the revival at Howard Payne described the formation of accountability groups. President Don Newbury said of the revival, "There was no pressure, no manipulation. The anointing of God was so evident." The press release began by saying, "The spring campus revival meeting at Howard Payne University actually became a revival experience."

GO HOME AND TELL

Tuesday, February 21. Today a woman came up to me and said, "I went to your church Sunday night. I have to tell you something. When I was a teenager, I was saved. I lived in Bangkok, and my family was Buddhist. I led six other girls to the Lord, and we started our own little church. Today it is the largest church of any denomination in all of Thailand. But I came to a better life in America. I was listening to Henry Blackaby. I had been through *Experiencing God*. God spoke to my heart and said, 'Do you remember when you touched those people, and I started this great church? All your family members are still lost. Your father tore up your Bible.' I must go back to my people and tell them about Jesus."

I have just been asked to share on March 1 at Southwestern Seminary. It is an overwhelming thought to share there. Although I have no idea what God might do or even if the campus is prepared for revival, I am excited about going.

HE TOUCHED ME

Monday, February 26. Yesterday morning our people had a deep time of prayer for the service at Southwestern. There was a sense of expectancy and the deep need to pray this week. I took some of our people with me to Greater Faith Community Church, a predominantly black church in our town. The pastor is a wonderful man named Aaron Blake. When we got there, we didn't know that a charismatic church was there as well. We had a joint service. In fact, there were several other churches there.

We had a three-and-a-half-hour service. This was another great experience in worship. I preached on how revival can solve the problems of racism. I told about how I was discipled by a black man in college and how I feel I need to have an impact in the area of racism.

In the service, there was a little eighty-seven-year-old black woman. At the prayer time at the altar, our minister of music reached over and took her hand. She began to worship loudly. She told us afterward that this was the first time a white man had ever touched her hand! We were able to hug her and rejoice with her. There was such healing and embracing going on all over. There was a deep sense that God was breaking through racial barriers. We found out our Hispanic mission had broken out in revival in the middle of the Lord's Supper service. We sense that God is using revival to break down racial barriers in our city.

SOUTHWESTERN SEMINARY

Fort Worth, Thursday, March 2. Early yesterday morning I went to Southwestern Seminary. As I prayed with President Hemphill, we sought revival for the campus. When we entered the packed chapel, I was amazed. People were out in the rotunda looking in. I shared the story of what God had done. We had been told that the day before, some of our Howard Payne students had shared in some of the classes. Some seminary students were so moved that they stayed up all night praying and fasting for revival. After I shared the story, the president allowed the students to stay beyond normal chapel time.

I simply said that if they wanted to come to the altar, they could. I sat down, and students began to come quietly to the altar. One girl cried out and said, "Lord, please send revival fire on us!" The students began to come, and come, and come.

They confessed all forms of sin—adultery, homosexuality, lust, pornography, greed, and racism. Every time students confessed, other students gathered around them, loved them, and prayed for them.

When the confessions finally ended, students continued to pray. As students went to their churches that evening, tremendous revival movements followed. I preached at Sagamore Hills that night; our service lasted more than three hours. Sleet was falling outside, but inside God was pouring out revival.

Brownwood, Monday, March 6. Yesterday was again a tremendous day. In the morning we had a time of joy and rejoicing in what God had done at Southwestern. God poured Himself out again with another lengthy service and invitation time. The *Baptist Standard,* the Texas Baptist state paper, will be carrying a story about Southwestern. Our adults are excited; our junior and senior high are also excited. Thirty high school students are meeting at lunchtime to pray and fast for continuing revival.

REVIVAL, DAD!

One of our parents thought his junior high student's prayer group ran too long, so he went to get his son. When he opened the door, he saw the junior high students on their knees praying. His son came to the door and said, "What do you want, Dad?" His dad said, "What's going on in there?" His son shrugged and said, "Uh, revival, Dad!" He turned around to go and pray some more.

It continues in our school in a powerful way! A principal from out of town called the principal of our high school, saying, "I've heard about this new program going on. How can we have it where we are?" He had to say it was not a program but a person—Jesus!

Yesterday morning the choir sang the song "I Stand in Awe of You." As they sang, spontaneously the congregation stood up. The choir began to cry! I began to cry! Everyone began to cry! I stood up to preach, crying. We had a tremendous prayer time before I could even preach. Sunday night we canceled our regular schedule and took our entire church through the revival prayer guide, which the deacons had been through. It walks the reader through the Sermon on the Mount. It was written by Christian Communicators Worldwide.

Then we opened up the microphones for more deep confession of sin. The principal of the high school confessed he had been unfaithful to the church. How could he be an example to the kids? Our men gathered around him in prayer. The chief of police knelt, recommitted his life, and confessed sin. People gathered around him for prayer. The Howard Payne basketball coach confessed sin, and others gathered around him. On and on it went to the end of this glorious service.

BEESON DIVINITY SCHOOL

Birmingham, Alabama, Wednesday, March 8. Chris Robeson and I went to speak at Beeson Divinity School. We had a tremendous time. Chris and I shared in chapel and classes. Chapel continued more than three hours, extending into class time. Once again there was deep confession of sin. Like Ken Hemphill at Southwestern and Don Newbury at Howard Payne, it seems that the openness of the leadership of the school is a key factor in whether or not revival comes. Dean Timothy George described what happened at Beeson as a spontaneous, significant movement of God's Spirit—a movement that he hopes will prepare for an even greater revival. At the students' request, Beeson scheduled a day of prayer and fasting to follow.

We shared also at First Baptist, Birmingham, as different churches came together. There was a real sense that God was working there. One student at Beeson, referring to those who oppose revival, said, "You know, sometimes when God lights a fire, some people stand too far away to get warm."

BLESSING IN THE BLANK SPOT

Brownwood, Monday, March 13. Sunday was another day of revival. God is spreading the word of this across the nation. We are hearing of revival in other colleges, including Olivet Nazarene in Illinois, campuses in Kentucky, Louisiana, and elsewhere.

The press continues to cover this. The *Fort Worth Star-Telegram* and the San Antonio newspapers are covering it. Radio programs are covering it, even in Dallas-Fort Worth. Our people continue to be overwhelmed at how God is working and spreading the word of what He has done.

A man named Ed came to our church recently on a Wednesday night in absolute misery. He couldn't even talk he was weeping so. We baptized him yesterday. He has given his life to the Lord and God has restored his marriage. Even his physical appearance is drastically different.

Again, yesterday, we were so overwhelmed that I couldn't preach until we prayed. We had about a ten-minute blank spot on the radio program because individuals were praying aloud in the congregation and couldn't be heard over the radio. I talked to the manager of the radio station and apologized for the blank spot. He said, "Don't worry about it. A woman called in during that blank spot. She said she had just turned on the station for the first time. She heard distant praying, murmuring, and the sound of crying. It so moved her that the Lord came into her heart right then. She wanted to know what church that was." God can move in a blank spot and bring someone to Him.

During both Sunday services, God seemed to open a new chapter of revival and ministry. We have churches and ministries coming from all over the state just to be in our services. When they call, we try to tell them that we are not doing anything special. God is simply present in an unusual way, and they continue to come. We began this past Sunday to gather these churches at the altar and pray for them as they go back home.

This is also the beginning of spring break. We have students going out to many places sharing the story. Invitations are flooding in for students and adults to come and tell what God has done in revival.

ILLINOIS CATCHES FIRE

O'Fallon, Illinois, Wednesday, March 15. Last night I went to Illinois to speak to the Illinois State Evangelism Conference. They had set this up less than a week ago, believing that after praying for revival ten years, this was the time. When I arrived to speak, I found out the preachers scheduled to preach that night had themselves canceled. They felt led of God to give the whole night to the message of revival.

I shared what God had done, and the Spirit of God poured Himself out on those pastors and state executives. As people confessed sin, the service lasted five hours. Churches reconciled with other churches; churches internally were reconciled. One pastor said, "I have spent thousands of hours on the phone talking about my disagreements with people in the state office," referring to people that were right there in the service. Then he confessed, "I haven't had a quiet time in three years." He gathered in repentance and prayer with the state director of evangelism and the executive director of Illinois.

People stood and cried aloud. We sang and praised the Lord. Three people from East St. Louis came up. They were gang members. They began to share and ask for prayer for East St. Louis. One of them said he had seen fifteen of his friends killed this past year. Now people were trying to kill him. He said, "I want to live, I just want to live." We committed to pray for the pastor who had gone to this gang-ridden area. We ended with pastors, gathered at the altar, joining in prayer and praise to God for the revival He had brought.

A CHURCH ON MISSION

Mexico, Thursday, March 16. I went from Illinois to Mexico to join our church's mission trip. It is amazing to see our young people share their faith. They are sharing Christ with people, building a church building, and teaching the people about evangelism. What a tremendous time!

Brownwood, Friday, March 17. We have returned from Mexico where our young people led almost one hundred people to Jesus. We are already hearing reports on the great things God is doing through our students on spring break and even our adults as they are sharing.

Monday, March 20. We had an incredible prayer time in our service yesterday morning. A Korean pastor came from Ft. Worth who is trying to reach the gangs. His two predecessors were murdered along with four others who were working in the effort there. People came to the altar and prayed for him. They wept for this man who has paid such a high price, while we have paid so little for revival.

WHEATON

Wheaton, Illinois, Friday, March 24. We now know that

what appears to be one of the greatest student movements on any campus in the history of our nation has taken place at Wheaton College this week. Two of our Howard Payne students, Jay Jones and Brandi Maguire, went to speak at Wheaton's invitation, and God poured Himself out there.

The service lasted all night on Sunday, and went through Thursday. There was deep confession and the putting away of sin—students were bringing pornography, alcohol and drugs, and putting them in garbage bags, literally to throw out their sin. Media has given it attention. A ninety-minute radio program was done with about ten of us from Howard Payne, Houston Baptist, Wheaton, and Southwestern Seminary. People from across the country heard about this. The word of revival spreads.

Many churches are entering into deep revival—reports from Florida, California, and Illinois. What God began in the evangelism conference in Illinois is spreading, particularly in Southern Illinois. In addition, revival is taking place in Louisiana, Houston, and San Antonio. Jersey Village Baptist Church of Houston had a four-hour service after two of our Howard Payne students shared.

LORD, TOUCH THE WORLD!

We are intensifying our prayer. A day of prayer and fasting is set-aside on Monday of each week to meet and pray during the lunch hour. We are praying that this will become a national spiritual awakening, touching campuses and churches across the nation.

Students went to Wayland Baptist University with our minister to students, Rick Cavitt. Another movement of

God came among the students there.

Monday, March 27. Yesterday was another wonderful day. Every Sunday is like that now. Yesterday morning Jay Jones shared about the Wheaton revival. What a powerful testimony! Many people from churches as far away as Mississippi came to be a part of what is happening.

We challenged our people to let the Lord deepen their own revival experience, that perhaps we were patting ourselves on the back and not moving deeper into revival ourselves. God spoke in a wonderful way. Once again we baptized as professions of faith continue every Sunday.

Sunday night I traveled to First Baptist in Seguin, where I had a commitment to do an evangelism rally. It was wonderful. Churches canceled their evening services and allowed me to share the story. We had a three-hour service, with confession of sin, brokenness, and prayer, followed by praise and worship.

KEEP ME FROM PRIDE!

God continues to open doors of opportunity to share. I'll be at Southern Seminary April 13 and Asbury April 14. Hearts are deeply burdened for the possibilities there. Already in the fall and the following spring there are other opportunities. God continues to deal with my heart in the area of pride, to be sure that I don't get in the way.

A few weeks ago, Donna and I did a retreat for Life Action Ministries. There was a tremendous outpouring among members of the staff and supporters of the ministry. Confession and brokenness continued for several hours. Byron Paulus, the head of that ministry, shared about the Welsh revival, when God had powerfully used Evan Roberts. Byron shared that Roberts was not used as powerfully in the latter part of his life. It seems that this began when some people wanted him to come out on a balcony to receive applause for all he had done. He did and was never again used to the level he had been before. That story frightened me so that I don't think I'll ever forget it.

Lord, keep me from ever being a victim of pride.

CHAPTER 4
THE POWER OF TESTIMONY

HOWARD PAYNE STUDENTS

Immediately following the revival at Howard Payne, many students and others began to go forth and share the story of the revival, often causing further revival fires to flame. Here are the testimonies of students and one administrator from Howard Payne University.

REND YOUR HEARTS

Chris Robeson [The Howard Payne University senior who read the Scripture when revival began at Coggin Avenue on January 22]

God in His sovereign grace chose to move upon the hearts of His children during the morning service on January 22, 1995, at Coggin Avenue Baptist Church. Over the last few years, the one common prayer of some college students and church members was a cry for God to send true revival. What happened on this day was a complete picture of 2 Chronicles 7:14: "If My people who are called by My name will humble themselves, and pray and seek My face and turn from their wicked ways, then I will hear from heaven, and will forgive their sin and heal their land."

On a normal Sunday morning, only a few college students attend the early service. Nothing unusual was planned for this service, yet a rather large group of university students was in attendance.

As I entered the front of the church building, the Father ushered me into His presence. I could feel the Spirit's holy presence. It was very evident to me that God desired to speak to me. I began to perspire. My heart began to beat as fast as when I first came to know the Lord as my Savior. I did not know exactly what the Father was trying to say to me, so I began to turn through the Bible, back and forth, back and forth. I eventually stopped at the Book of Joel. As I scanned through the chapters, I came across a subtitle that said, "Rend Your Heart." I was brought face to face with the reality of the depth of my own sin and how much it hurt the Lord. I almost jumped out of my seat!

A battle began to rage in my heart. Not only was God speaking to me, He was leading me to make this declaration before the whole church body. I hesitated. I was so afraid of sharing something from my own heart that I almost missed the heart of God.

The time came for the invitation. I quickly walked to the front and met my pastor, Dr. John Avant. I knew that if God were leading me to share with the church, He would lay it on his heart. I asked for permission, and he said yes.

It is a miracle that my pastor understood what I said. By this time I had begun to shake tremendously. I stood before the church and turned to Joel 2:12. As I began to share, the weight of what I was about to say broke me. I did not know how the people would respond. I gathered my emotions and shared what I believed to be God's Word to all of us: "Rend your hearts!" It has become clear to me that God was desiring to show us just how far away from Him our hearts had gone. For a while I was the only one at the altar. I began to weep bitterly over my own sin and the state of my worship in God's sight. Soon an older lady came before the church and made a plea for prayer. One by one, college students began to respond in brokenness. Soon, the altar was filled with students and adults.

As time passed, it became clear that God's Spirit had not lifted and still desired to move upon the hearts of the people. Our pastor asked those who felt it necessary to leave for Sunday school to do so. Some left. Others went and brought back to the auditorium their entire Sunday school class. Our college minister brought the university students over in response to the pastor's request. There was not a break between the two services. For a long time, people wept before the Lord.

Each time I recall this specific service, I know that God was freeing me of some deep bitterness and beginning a process of renewal and revival.

THE PLUMB LINE

Jay Jones [Jay, a senior, was the first to testify on Tuesday night,
February 14, when revival came to Howard Payne. This testimony was shared
March 13 at First Baptist, Corinth, Texas.]

For four years I have heard about revival. People kept saying revival is coming! It's coming! But my heart grew bitter hearing about it. When I stepped on campus this semester, something was different. God was touching our campus. On Thursday evening, January 26, I went to a thing called University Celebration. People stood up and shared what God was doing. Singing, worship, and sharing started at 7:30 and continued two hours. It was incredible. People mentioned that God was working in revival. This time, my heart was not bitter and cold. I thought, *Yeah, God is doing a mighty work.* I went back the next Thursday. It was something—people just shared what God was doing.

On Sunday, Henry Blackaby came to the campus as the preacher for our spring revival. Blackaby pointed out that we could get so caught up in the things we're doing—the things we have, broken relationships, and families that are about to break up—that we neglect our relationship with God.

God began to show me problems in my own life. Amos 7:7 talks about God's plumb line. I took the plumb line and held it up to my life to see if it was straight. I thought, *Hey, I'm doing pretty good.* That's because I was using my own plumb line, not the plumb line of Jesus.

When I took the plumb line of Jesus, God showed me the way I was treating women. I thought, *I'm not having sex with them, so I'm OK.* I didn't break certain standards or barriers, but I thought, *You've got to be able to have a little fun, right?* God said, "Unacceptable. These are women of God, and I expect you to treat them that way."

God began to deal with pride, arrogance, and pettiness in my life. He allowed us during that time on Tuesday night, after several of us shared, to see Him move in a mighty way. I was the first to confess. At first I reasoned, "How can I get up and say what I have done wrong? I am a senior, a leader. People look up to me. People think I'm a good Christian." God said, "Don't worry about their judgment, worry about My judgment."

Henry Blackaby says the most solemn day of judgment will not be when God shows us what we did wrong: The most solemn day of judgment will be when He shows us what we could have been. Think of when God nudged your heart. You knew you needed to change, you needed to adjust something, but you didn't. Second Chronicles 7:14 is still true. It starts with prayer. I know some have been praying a long time. Some have felt God touch their hearts but have said, "Not yet, I'll get around to it sometime." When God nudges you, do what He tells you to do.

ON FIRE FOR GOD

Marty Webb [This senior also shared at Corinth, Texas.]

I work with the youth at Coggin, where Dr. Avant serves as pastor. Every Wednesday is amazing. God is moving mightily among the junior and senior high school students. They are on fire for God! Our junior high kids started meeting outside in the school hall to pray. The senior high students skip lunch. Twenty to thirty of them come together and pray for their lost friends. This is something that can't be explained. It's totally God. Yes, these kids are on fire and have really caught a vision, but it is just totally God. They have seen what happens when God changes a life.

We had our *Disciple Now* this past month. We began praying for some of their friends. On the next Wednesday, one of the girls for whom we had been praying was present. Three or four girls rushed up to me saying, "Marty, Marty, Jennifer just came to us and asked us to witness to her." God began to show me that if you are totally sold out, you will shine like Moses did when he came face to face with God. None of this can happen without brokenness. I must confess that I am very prideful. I want to be independent, but God is breaking me of that.

Once while reading Jesus' words, "'Whomever falls on that stone [Christ] will be broken; but on whomever it falls, it will grind him to powder'" (Luke 20:18). I had written a question mark in my Bible beside that verse because I did not understand it. The other day, I came across this passage again. It was amazing how God revealed to me what it means. If we fall on Christ, He is going to break us—our pride, arrogance, our unwillingness, and apparent shyness. When I say, "I am not like that, God; I am not outgoing; I can't go and share with them," all of the walls that I have will be broken to pieces. But the second part of the verse says if the Rock falls on you, it will grind you to powder. My prayer is that no one will incur the judgment of Christ because of disobedience. If you do not do God's will, He will fall upon you. He will judge you. You will incur His wrath. That is the way God is. He tells you to move.

I urge you to become broken before God, not emotional! Yes, if emotions come, so be it. But brokenness is more than crying your eyes out. Brokenness is turning from your sin, choosing not to do it again. That is where brokenness begins. It is admitting what is going on and being honest with yourself. That was my problem, and I am sure many others have that problem too. You still may not be able to admit sin to yourself. It is really hard. You try to talk yourself out of it. You say, "Oh, no, it is not that bad." But no, sin is sin; and it grieves the heart of God. Brokenness comes when you say, "I am nothing." Then God says, "But I see you through the blood of Christ."

God will not send revival to stiff-necked people.

Throughout the Old Testament, He referred to the Israelites' having stiff necks; and He broke them. If we have stiff necks and are stubborn against His will, He will break us.

BROKENNESS

Bill Fishback [Bill is vice president of Financial Affairs at Howard Payne University and a member of Coggin Avenue Baptist Church.]

Going to church had become hard for me. I found myself crying in my Bible study class and in our worship services, but I was not sure why. Something made me very uncomfortable with myself, and tears were my only response. I was embarrassed. I am forty-two years old, and I've been in church all my life. I was really bothered by being moved to tears in front of my family and friends.

Sunday, January 22, was another one of those days. As we opened our Bible study, my friend Terry asked to share an announcement from our pastor. Terry had been to the early service and said something unusual was going on in the sanctuary, something he could not explain. He said there seemed to be an unusual moving of the Holy Spirit in the service and there was a sense of "brokenness." I did not hear anything else for a few moments as I began to weep.

That word **brokenness!** Terry said a university student had addressed the congregation during the invitation time about our need to be "broken" over sin in our lives as God called us to holiness.

Brokenness—that was it! Though I had been a Christian for years, I now realized the Holy Spirit had been dealing with me about unconfessed sin in my life. It was destroying my fellowship with God and with others that I loved.

As we entered the sanctuary, people were praising the Lord in song and praying at the altar. The pastor reported what had been going on and that he could not explain it. God was doing an unusual work among our people.

I stood by the choir and cried miserably until I joined others at the altar to ask God's forgiveness for hidden sins. Only God and I knew about these sins, but they were wrecking my life. Three young men from Howard Payne asked if they could pray with me. We shared a wonderful time of seeking God's forgiveness at the altar.

As we left that morning I was somewhat relieved—little did I know what was to come. For the next few weeks, I had an uneasy peace about having "confessed my sins" that Sunday.

Howard Payne University's annual spring revival began on February 13. As Henry Blackaby spoke, I sensed he had an unusual anointing from God. He preached with simplicity but with great clarity and power. On Tuesday evening Henry preached from Matthew 16:13-25, and asked, "Is He the Christ in your life?" He said we were at a "watershed moment" in our lives as we decide if He really is Lord in our lives! I thought, *Jesus not only wants to be my Savior but also my Lord. Because He is the Christ, He has the right to rule my life. When He is Lord of my life, my life will show it. I proclaim Him with my life and my words—one way or the other!* I knew my life was not proclaiming Christ as Lord because of that unconfessed sin.

The service and invitation lasted almost four hours. About 150 students and adults came forward to pray and confess specific sins to God and the entire assembly. Many asked those who listened to hold them accountable in the future for their sins. In those prayer groups, I had to confess my secret sin.

As many men, young and old, confessed this same sin, I realized I was not alone in this battle with Satan for my thought life. I knew I was being so consumed by evil desires that I was a living fraud before God, before my wife and sons, and before my friends. It was destroying me inside. The morning I confessed my sin in our Bible study department was the day I finally asked God to forgive me of this sin.

I have shared this confession with my wife, with a university fraternity I sponsor, and with my accountability group. Letting God take that burden from me was one of the most difficult experiences I have had as a Christian—and one of the most wonderful. I was finally desiring holiness in my life.

I had often wanted a quiet time with God, but my schedule was always such that I never made time for Him. The next morning, I was awake at 5:00 A.M. with an incredible desire to pray and seek God. My alarm is still set for 6:00 A.M., but I am awake at 5:00 most mornings.

I have discovered for the first time in my life the joy of prayer and time alone with my Father. Seeing Him answer my prayers builds my faith.

Could I say that I have not been tempted since? That would be a lie. Attacks began immediately. Every day I face this battle. But now I know my Lord can strengthen me to turn away from temptation and seek Him instead. A Christian friend said, "Bill, you can't keep a vulture from flying over your head, but you can keep it from building a nest in your hair." The temptations are there everyday—on TV, the magazine covers at the grocery checkout, everywhere I turn. Now that Christ reigns as Lord in my life, the "nest" that would destroy me now is gone.

RELATIONSHIPS

A Male Junior at Howard Payne [Also at Corinth]

When I first arrived at Howard Payne, my roommate, John, and I became close friends. About three months into the semester, something happened. Our friendship began to deteriorate. We stopped talking to each other, doing things together, and became bitter toward each other. Our pride would not allow us to reconcile. Because of this, I moved in with another roommate. Over the three and a half years since that experience, we never really talked.

I began praying for this revival. I really desired a work of God! I especially wanted to experience God in my own life, to sense His presence around me, and know what was happening to me was because He was there, guiding me.

In the January 22 service at Coggin Avenue, Dr. Avant emphasized revival as a part of the preparation for the arrival of Henry Blackaby. During the invitation, I felt led to go to the altar. This was a big step for me because I hadn't been to the altar in many years. My pride had kept me from going because I thought, *as long as I can sit here in my pew, I don't have to go forward. I can get things right with God right where I am.* God so worked in my life that before I could even think about it, I was weeping at the altar. God's presence became so unbelievably real to me.

During the revival on campus, which was two weeks later, my pride started to emerge again. I went to every revival service, and at every revival service there was an altar call. As students were getting their lives right with God, I sat in my seat and thought, I *don't have to get things right. I am a junior. A lot of people look up to me. I don't have to let them know that things are not right with God in my life.*

On Tuesday night, Henry Blackaby brought a message about urgency. He shared with us a passage that really convicted my heart. Hebrews 10:26 says, "For if we sin willfully after we have received the knowledge of the truth, there no longer remains a sacrifice for sins." Jesus died and paid for our sins with His blood. There is no greater sacrifice that can be paid for our sins.

He also shared Hebrews 10:29: "Of how much worse punishment, do you suppose, will he be thought worthy who has trampled the Son of God underfoot, counted the blood of the covenant by which he was sanctified a common thing, and insulted the Spirit of grace?" Once we receive that truth and willingly go against God in sin, we trample on the name of Jesus Christ. It became so real to me that sin is something that really truly grieves God.

As I sat in the service Tuesday night, I listened to many students as they shared. I felt the need to go forward, but my pride emerged again. I reasoned with myself, *you don't have to go to the altar. All those guys are testifying. But you can just sit right here, confess, and everything will be all right.*

Once again, God propelled me forward. As I looked around where I sat, the seats were empty. Everyone had gone to the stage. I started walking up to the altar. When I arrived at the stage, I did not know what to expect, or even why I went. At this point, there were probably one hundred people on stage.

I was stepping around people, and then I spotted John, my former roommate, at the back of the stage. He had tears in his eyes. At that point, I knew why God had led me forward. It was time to restore a relationship that had been bitter and sour for more than three years. Previously, I was too proud to go and tell him, "I am sorry, John." As we approached one another, we embraced, cried, and prayed on each other's shoulders. We prayed that God would break our pride and not let it be a barrier in our relationship again. I felt peace come over me like a shower as my heart was cleansed. We must have prayed for fifteen to twenty minutes.

As I left the stage, I found other people with whom I had bitter relationships and where things were not right. God began bringing to my mind those things that were wrong in my life. I had lust, bitterness, and things that I did not consider bad sins. In my rationale, they were OK. Surely, God did not consider them that bad. Then God said, "You are trampling on My name." I was so broken that I just knelt, wept, and prayed. As God continued to make known to me the sins of my life, I was to confess them one by one.

God was so real as people were getting their lives right with Him and with each other. There was a great peace and joy in the lives of everyone in the room. You could just feel God's presence. It was real, very real!

I really prayed during the next few days. I really prayed that this would be more than a temporary emotional experience. I prayed that God would continue the revival and that more students would come to know this joy in their hearts.

During these past couple of days, we have had an event on campus we call "Spring Sing." People do different acts for the preview weekend, which is for prospective students who are visiting the campus. Previously, I had participated in two "Spring Sing." The competition had been contemptuous. Organizations demonstrated less than Christian attitudes as they competed for the prize given to the winning performance. This year we really prayed for "Spring Sing." There were six organizations that did acts. At the end of "Spring Sing," after all the acts were done, all the students met on stage. They embraced, not with the organizations, but with everyone. Arm in arm, with tears in their eyes, they sang "Undivided." For the students who had been there in the past, it was really touching. This was evidence to me that God was still working on the Howard Payne campus, and still working in the lives of students. I encountered a couple of roommates from last year who had transferred and had come back. In tears, I embraced both of them on stage. They said, "It has changed so much." God is powerful. Many lives have been changed on our campus. Every week we hear of more stories about students going out and revivals emerging. This is evidence of answered prayer.

OBEDIENCE

Tim Williams. [Tim is a junior at HPU. He and Richard Robeson spent a week in March sharing in Houston. This testimony was given at Bay brook Baptist Church, Friendswood, south of Houston, March 15.]

When I went to Howard Payne as a freshman, I saw

problems at the school, like other schools. I prayed, "Lord, I need some friends I can pray with." The Lord began to bring friends into my life, including Richard Robeson. We started praying together, sharing our struggles.

As school began this spring, there was anticipation about what God was going to do with the students. Spontaneous prayer began on campus. About thirty or forty students, mostly freshman and sophomores, gathered on Friday night. They worshiped and praised the Lord. They called these meetings "Jesus Parties." I was at one that went until 1:00 A.M. I thought it was strange that college students would give up Friday nights to worship God. I was moved by that and by seeing the Lord orchestrate other things that usually set up a spiritual awakening.

The closer February 13 came—the first day of the Blackaby revival meeting—the more people prayed. Not all the students were on their knees, but there was a core group.

Sunday evening, February 12, Dr. Blackaby spoke at my home church, Coggin Avenue Baptist. I felt convicted, about nothing in particular. I just felt bad.

Monday we had chapel, and the sermon was cutting to the heart. I realized who I was when I lived outside of Christ. Monday night came with the same result. Tuesday morning came, and the same feeling—I just felt bad. A prayer meeting was called by word of mouth for 6:00 P.M. I prayed for a while with a group of about fifteen, but it seemed so dry. I felt dirty. I thought to myself, *I'm good! I pray! I even fast! I know I'm a Christian!* I couldn't understand why I felt so bad. This was supposed to be revival. What happened to "The joy of the Lord is my strength?"

I left the prayer group and went to a corner to pray on my knees. "What is hindering me from experiencing revival?" I sensed the Lord say, "Remember Sunday night? A young man confessed sin. You need to do the same thing, only confess your own sin."

"No," I reasoned, "I'm not going to get up in front of seven hundred people and confess my struggles." I sensed that I could either confess and obey, or not, at which time God would pass me by. I was scared.

After fifteen minutes of debating, I got up and sat on the second row. It was about 6:45. People were still praying. I started flipping through my Bible. I came across a verse I already knew: James 5:16: "Confess your trespasses to one another, and pray for one another, that you may be healed. The effectual, fervent prayer of a righteous man avails much." As I read that, I was cut again, for this was like confirmation of what God was calling me to do.

As the service began, I sat there. Once again, the standard was laid down. I felt bad. As the service came to what I thought was the close, Henry said, "We have two students who need to share." One was my roommate, Richard Robeson, and the other was a good friend, Jay. They got up and confessed. The things they confessed were the very things I was dealing with. As they spoke, my heart was beating, I knew this was my opportunity. As Richard gave the microphone to Henry, I ran up on stage, grabbed, it, and read the verse from James. I shared my sin and asked for prayer—the lust of the eyes had plagued us and kept us from going to the next level. As the three of us shared, it seemed as though the Holy Spirit rushed in like the wind. As I spoke I trembled, not for fear of rejection but because of the power of God.

Henry addressed the body concerning how to respond to sin appropriately. I was broken for my sin and for the Christians at Howard Payne. I believe almost one hundred men came forward confessing pride. Women then came and confessed also.

It was such a cleansing process, and finally it came to a close. I saw many things come as a result. Many relationships have been healed. Reconciliation has come among churches and among college students.

On Monday, March 6, I was in our library typing a paper. A student named Mark walked by. We greeted each other casually. The Lord touched my heart with this thought: "You need to forgive him, and you need to ask his forgiveness." Mark was arrogant. He liked to argue, and we had not gotten along. I immediately prayed, "Oh, Lord, I'm sorry. Please forgive me." And I knew that was not enough because Mark did not hear my confession.

I sought him out. When we met, I told him I needed to speak to him. I said, "I'm sorry our relationship has been rocky, and that there has been malice." He said, "I forgive you, and I'm really glad you sought me out. Last night during my quiet time I was praying, 'Lord, why am I missing Your work?' So, I made of list of people with whom I have had problems. I realized the problem was not with other people, but with me. The Lord has led me to get right with all of these people. I'm glad you sought me out, Tim, it would take me a while to get to the W's [Williams].

It is amazing to see how the Lord has worked in a divine way to bring about reconciliation. Revival is a lifestyle—a lifestyle of obedience.

CHAPTER 5
A HOWARD PAYNE
STUDENT'S JOURNAL

BRANDI MAGUIRE

Brandi was a communications major at Howard Payne University and a member of Coggin Avenue Baptist Church. She describes herself as "just an ordinary college student, "but these jottings from her diary tell the story of an extraordinary semester in her junior year.

My story is not about Brownwood or Howard Payne. I do want to tell you what God is doing there in order to brag on my Lord. My life and the lives of many of my friends have been changed forever. This is not because of a place, for God is bigger than places.

On January 22 we had a service that we could not easily end. There was no Sunday school. We kept praying, praising the Lord, and seeking God's face. People were really experiencing the presence of God.

Two weeks later, we had a *Disciple Now* for junior high, high school, and college students. I grew up in church. I grew up learning to pray for revival. My pastors said, "Pray! Pray for revival! Pray that God will send it!" I prayed, but I never knew what I was praying about. I just prayed for it because that was what my pastor taught. Then, for the first time I, with others, laid on a carpet for a whole weekend with our faces on the floor and sought God. Second Chronicles 16:9 gripped all of us: "For the eyes of the Lord run to and fro throughout the whole earth, to show Himself strong on behalf of those whose heart is loyal to Him."

Unless we fully, absolutely, completely commit our hearts to the Lord, we will never find Him the way that He desires for us to find Him. God says: "And you will seek Me and find Me, when you search for Me with all your heart" (Jer. 29:13).

Seeking Him with our whole heart! That's what we have done in Brownwood as university students. We got up in the morning and sought the Lord. We went to class and sought the Lord. We went to chapel and did not want to leave. Between classes, we prayed with each other. Jesus Parties began happening all over. We began calling people saying, "Come over, we are just going to praise and worship the Lord. If it lasts all night, then it lasts all night." That's what we are doing. That is how we are spending our Friday and Saturday nights.

We are doing mission projects. We want to go and share. That's what it's all about. It is not about staying within the church walls and thinking, "This is so awesome! God is bringing revival to this church." It is about going out and telling other people. If God sends revival to your church, my prayer is that you call your friends and relatives and say, "Can we come to your church and share what the Lord is doing? God called us to go out and preach His word to all the nations." Believe me, I am not a preacher, but I am telling about the Lord. We need to go out and tell what the Lord is doing.

A breaking point for our university came on Tuesday night in our revival service. Henry Blackaby was with us from Sunday through Wednesday. On Tuesday morning he said that every time we sin is like taking Jesus, laying Him on the ground, and stomping on His face—stomping all over someone who died for us. That was really convicting for a lot of people.

After a lot of prayer that night, Henry Blackaby called two students forward. One, a ministerial student, said, "I want you to know, I'm standing before you, my peers, teachers, president, and pastor. I'm lusting! I'm sinning! I have impurities in my heart!" Instantly, guys flooded to the stage—"I do too," "I do too," "I do too!" Girls went up and said, "You know what? The reason you have impurities in your life is the way we dress. And we're guilty, and we're sorry."

The floor of the auditorium was filled with people confessing their sins. The amazing thing is that I don't remember the sins that were mentioned that night. That's not what was important. What was important was that they confessed their sins, got right with their Lord, and now He's working in our lives.

We had just become one. People who had never been friends became friends. We saw football players and band members praying together. We just don't normally see that. It's revival! It's from the Lord! And we praise Him for that.

Here are notes about my experiences taken from my journal.

HEARTBEAT WEEKEND

Friday through Sunday, February 3-5, 1995. God wants me to have an intimate relationship with Him. Fifteen minutes a day just is not enough. I experienced God this weekend at our *Disciple Now* like I never have before. We spent hours in prayer, on our faces. We sought God with all our hearts and *we found Him!!!* God is beginning a work in the lives of Howard Payne University students.

Tuesday, February 14. We began our scheduled university revival services with Henry Blackaby. The Tuesday evening service began at 7:00 and ended at 11:00! A time of confession, repentance, crying, hurting, prayer, encouragement, and celebration! God is revealing Himself to us more and more everyday—it is awesome! All that I know is that several of my friends are getting right with the Lord, and I am so excited. I am praying that the Lord will use me. I want to be a vessel for Him. Whatever I have to do, I am willing.

FIRST BAPTIST CHURCH, HOUSTON, TEXAS

Sunday, February 26. This weekend I went home and attended my church, First Baptist, Houston. Surprisingly to me, I was asked to share this morning by pastor John Bisagno at the end of the church service. It was totally the Lord. I was brief and to the point; I didn't want to take advantage of my time! After church, a man came up to me and told me that he attended Howard Payne in 1949 and that he had been praying for forty-six years that God would touch the heart of someone there like his was touched. My heart has definitely been touched and is continuing to be. I am so thankful!

JERSEY VILLAGE BAPTIST CHURCH, HOUSTON

Sunday Night, February 26. Kelly Parrish [now Brandi's husband!] and I spoke at Jersey Village. God was already at work there! I told them I felt like I was at home. Dr. Alvin Reid invited Kelly and me to share. When we walked through the church doors, we felt like we were experiencing exactly what was happening in Brownwood. This was just another assurance for me to know that the Lord is faithful and in control. He is bigger than doing something just in one place.

God is so good. He broke hearts and then mended them in a way that was incredible. Families were reunited and teenagers were loved on in beautiful ways. God is teaching me that He is bigger than Brownwood. He will be anywhere that we invite Him to be.

I tried to encourage everyone there. I told them, "There is still a lot of work to be done at Howard Payne and in Brownwood, but we've started. So have you from what I understand." I spoke directly to the youth: "I would encourage you youth to stay strong in the Lord and in service to Him. If you're not walking with God in purity, get pure right now.

Just one of you could change your whole school. If I could encourage you in any way, it would be to come clean before the Lord. If you don't get right with the Lord, then there is no way you are going to see Him work in a complete way."

Thank You, Lord, for allowing me to share what You alone are doing!

FIRST BAPTIST CHURCH, SUNDOWN, TEXAS

Sunday, March 12. Kelly and I (my fiancé Kelly as of last night!) spoke in Sunday school to a group of youth and then in the service for First Baptist in Sundown. The people have an incredible hunger for the Lord. The youth were on their faces seeking God and crying out to Him. The Spirit of the Lord was so thick in the place that we could not speak without crying. It was very special. Several people flooded to the altar to pray, and several confessed disobedience to God. Their hearts were so broken. God is beginning a great work in this church. Revival is about to take place.

WHEATON COLLEGE, ILLINOIS

Sunday, March 19. Jay and I were invited to share with students about what God is doing at Brownwood. The program began at 7:30 P.M. It was incredible. Immediately students rushed to the front to confess sin. Students everywhere are realizing that the judgment of God is more important than the judgment of their friends. At 6:00 A.M. we asked students to go home because of exhaustion. The decision was made to meet again that night. Sins of lust, pornography, pride, disobedience, hate, unforgiveness, homosexuality, and stealing were all confessed.

Monday, March 20. We started at 9:30 P.M. and continued until 2:00 A.M. Five garbage bags were filled with things that students felt were stumbling blocks. Examples are CDs, magazines of all kinds, alcohol, drugs, roses (representing old relationships), and several other things.

Why has God chosen me to be here? I feel like I am so unworthy. I am honored! I am scared! I am intimidated! I am excited!! I'm just an ordinary college student with an extraordinary God!

NORTH METRO FELLOWSHIP CHURCH, DENTON, TEXAS

Sunday, March 26. Kelly and I arrived here on Saturday night and talked with the pastor for a while. He was worried about the spiritual condition of the youth. He had been praying for the Lord to move in his church. On Sunday morning we prayed with him and went to share with these teenagers. The minute we walked into the room the youth were silent and stared at us. Kelly and I shared and then opened it up to a time of questions.

Students began to ask how they could be examples at school and why was it so hard. The only thing that I knew to tell them was that Jesus suffered so much that He was put to death. They needed to be willing to suffer a little bit for Him. We asked them to bow their heads and raise their hands if they were not Christians. One boy did, and he accepted Christ right there. We were so excited! The service started at 10:45. Kelly and I had the whole service to share. The presence of God was so thick in the place that I could not speak without crying. The Lord broke hearts of the youth and adults that morning and the service did not end until 1:30. There were four people saved, one for whom his family had been praying for several years. It was a wonderful experience.

GORDON COLLEGE, WENHAM, MASSACHUSETTS

Wednesday, April 5. At 7:30 p.m. Chris Robeson and I, along with Matt Yarrington from Wheaton, shared with some students who had been praying for revival. As we prayed with them, their hearts began to break. They confessed sin until 9:15 as they renewed commitments with the Lord. It was a very powerful time. At 10:00, we shared at a meeting that all students were asked to attend. It was not mandatory, but about five hundred students showed up anyway. A time of confession took place that lasted until 3:00 A.M. It was so different. Some of the people who were present had hearts that were so hard that it took a while before a true brokenness was seen. God was very gentle. I have never sensed something so tender before. There was a strange quietness. The only sounds were the almost inaudible crying and weeping of the students. It was sweet.

EASTERN NAZARENE COLLEGE, SOUTH BOSTON, MASSACHUSETTS

Thursday, April 6. Chapel began at 9:50. We were told that forty students had stayed up all night praying for the service and thirty-five more had come early that morning to pray. Chris spoke after a song, "Embrace the Cross." He invited students to come to the altar if they felt like they needed to embrace the cross that morning.

After Chris spoke, I shared about the junior high and high school students in Brownwood. I told them how excited these students are about living for Jesus. I also read a letter from a junior high girl about what God was doing, and I shared about my experience at Jersey Village. Matt went to the microphone at 10:35. It was time for chapel to be over. He told the students that they were free to leave and that he would not be offended. But only two students left of the three hundred. When Matt was finished, the students began to flood to the stage and weep. It was beautiful. God really showed me that religion does not matter. He is who matters and that is all!

Chris and I began to pray for the faculty of the school. Not long after that, the president of the school came in and announced that classes had been canceled and that students and faculty were being encouraged to come and see what God was doing. We got to share with the faculty about our broken hearts and challenged them to be not only teachers to the students but also to be their friends and mentors. As we left at 1:30, students were flooding into the chapel to see what God was doing. It was exciting and precious to see once again the Lord do what He desires most in the hearts of His people.

I have never been happier in all my life. God is

teaching me new things everyday about living for Him and sacrificing for Him, but it is all so worth it. I would not trade this time in my life for anything in the world. My GPA is not going to matter in five, ten, or even twenty years but the souls of the people with whom I share will matter for all eternity. I pray everyday that the Lord will use me and that I will be pleasing to Him. I figure that the least I can do is live my life for Him because He lived His life knowing that someday He would die for me. He who began a good work in me will be faithful to complete it. I pray that I will be faithful to fulfill that promise!!

FIRST BAPTIST CHURCH, HOUSTON, TEXAS

Friday, April 14. Wow! I spoke at an all-day solemn assembly at my home church. More than twelve hundred people! This was an incredible opportunity for me because my heart is here the most. These are the people who taught me about the Lord, here where I grew up. I told them the Lord had laid on my heart that I needed their help and their prayers because I'm just a normal college student trying to honor God. It was the hardest place for me to speak because I knew them so well. I had a break for much of April. I needed it! Lots of schoolwork to catch up on.

CHICO STATE UNIVERSITY AND SIMPSON COLLEGE IN CALIFORNIA

Friday, May 5. Kelly and I went to northern California with Dr. Avant, who spoke at a pastor's conference there. We spoke at Chico State University, which has about 14,000 students. Only five hundred are Christians, we were told. All the Christian organizations came together for us to speak.

Saturday, May 6. After that we went to Simpson College in San Francisco. This school had already dismissed for the summer, but the local churches came together to hear us. After we shared, those who came broke into groups to pray. It was beautiful the way the Lord began to break the hearts of the people.

God is teaching me that revival can come in different ways. Not everyone has to confess in a large group setting. Some can find release by confessing in a small group. Lord, You are so much bigger than we are! The service went from 10:00 A.M. to past 1:30 P.M.

CHICO, CALIFORNIA

Sunday, May 7. Kelly and I went to two different churches. I went to the largest church in Chico, much bigger than Coggin Avenue. The pastor gave me the entire early service. People began to flood down the aisles. This was much deeper than Friday night had been. The early service turned into the late service. We started at 8:00 A.M. and continued until 1:15 P.M. People came broken, crying.

OROVILLE, CALIFORNIA

Sunday night. All churches from every denomination came to hear us share. Incredible! The Spirit was there! The Lord broke my heart as I shared. I was filled with tears. He is teaching me how to hurt with people. I shared about my time with the faculty at Eastern Nazarene College. I told my burden for some of our faculty in Brownwood. When I sat down, it was quiet for ten minutes. Then, a man confessed sin. People ministered to him. Another fifteen minutes went by. People were quietly dealing with the Lord. Then another spoke. For two and a half hours we continued. They were dealing with the Lord!

God has truly worked in my life in the past four months. I have learned to hear His voice—to know when He is at work in a place and when He is not.

God is teaching me the importance of humility. He has made Philippians 4:13 come alive: "I can do all things through Christ who strengthens me." The Lord has also taught me discipline. My grades actually went up this semester, even with all the travel! I'm also learning the discipline of saying no. At one point I became ill with strep throat—so ill the doctor told me he would put me in the hospital to get some rest. Yet I was still having people call and at times plead for me to speak. I can't bring revival! Only God does. I'm learning to pace myself.

I have experienced the world in its realness. I see what a hold Satan has on it. This is a big world, much bigger than my small town filled with churches! I pray daily that this is the beginning of the Lord's taking back what is His.

I wouldn't trade this semester of my life for anything in the world. At Howard Payne's graduation, I shared Philippians 1:6: "Being confident of this very thing, that He who has begun a good work in you will complete it until the day of Jesus Christ." The Lord will complete it. I want to be as faithful to Him.

CHAPTER 6
A HIGHWAY OF HOLINESS

HENRY BLACKABY
[The following is an abridged version of the message
Henry Blackaby delivered at the National
Convocation on Revival in Little Rock on February
16, 1995, the day after closing his meetings at
Howard Payne University.]

"A highway shall be there, and a road, and it shall be called the Highway of Holiness. The unclean shall not pass over it, but it shall be for others . . . But the redeemed shall walk there" (Isa. 35:8-9).

There was an awesome moment when God spoke to Isaiah. He spoke of a moment when He will establish a Highway of Holiness. God has not changed His agenda. Holiness is still a highway for God.

In late 1994 through early 1995, I watched the Lord create a Highway of Holiness in my own life—a highway over which He is passing.

HOLINESS AND REVIVAL

During the revival at Howard Payne, we spent four awesome days in the presence of God where holiness was very evident. Most who were in His presence absolutely could not stand without instantly confessing enormous sin in settings that would not be normal for them.

I watched on Sunday night, February 12, as twenty churches of various denominations spontaneously closed their services and joined us at Coggin Avenue Baptist Church. If you were to ask them, they would be unable to tell you why they came. At that invitation, extended spontaneously, there was great weeping and brokenness before the Lord. Even though they came across all denominational lines, we were one people with a terrible sense of what it means to stand in the presence of a holy God.

In God's presence all sin is exposed. Wherever else you may be, you are not in the presence of God unless sin is being exposed. You may be practicing religion, but you will know it when you are standing in the presence of a holy God. God takes the Word as a sword. In the hand of the His Spirit, the Word divides the bone and marrow and lays you instantly exposed to a holy God.

When God creates a Highway of Holiness, He exposes sin like a refiners' fire.

We had a noon luncheon on Tuesday, February 14. It was filled with business people and others—more than twenty different denominational groups. We were just about to close. Wisely, Pastor John Avant asked, "Before the benediction, is there anyone who feels the need to confess sin?" Some pastors began to cry out, "O God, my mind is so full of filth! My heart is so full of sin and lust!" They began to cry out. We were still standing there waiting to finish. People from all over the room acknowledged that they had sinned grievously against God. I waited a long time to talk to people.

A woman with two canes looked at me with tears. She said, "I'm eighty-eight years old and I desire purity toward God above all else, Do you think God could use me at eighty-eight?" I said to her, "Young lady, God is going to give you the best days of your life. God is creating a Highway of Holiness for you." She said, "Oh, I desire holiness more than anything else in the world."

If I were to bear witness to you to anything I see happening, it is that God is creating a Highway of Holiness. I say it with all the reverence of my soul: "the unclean shall not pass over it." It is for others—for those who understand the awesome holiness of God.

Our generation has little if any reference point in experiencing revival and almost no reference point to experience the holiness of God. You cannot talk about the holiness of God without at the same time having the refiner's fire touch every corner of your life and leave it absolutely exposed to Him. When you read the Word of God, it is like a hammer. The Word of God is like a blaze—everything in your heart and life is exposed. The Holy God does not play games.

ACCOUNTABILITY—PSALM 24

I have begun to sense with increasing intensity that the highway over which God comes is a Highway of Holiness. I've had a heart cry for revival since I was a lad. We need to apply Psalm 24 to revival praying:

Who may ascend into the hill of the Lord?
Or who may stand in His holy place?
He who has clean hands and a pure heart,
who has not lifted up his soul to an idol,
nor sworn deceitfully.
He shall receive blessing from the Lord
and righteousness from the God of his salvation.
Psalm 24:3-5

I am deeply convinced that all revival praying is an offense to God if we do not have a clean heart. It is almost blasphemy to ask a holy God to bless us when our hearts are unclean before Him. Revival praying has a prerequisite. Read it carefully: "Who can ascend into the hill of the Lord? Or who shall stand in His holy place?"

One of the greatest hindrances to revival and awakening is this: We do not hold ourselves accountable. We read the Word of God but do not hold ourselves accountable to see it implemented in our lives.

A pastor stands before his deacons knowing they have absolutely no sense of the holiness of God. They stand in this pastor's presence but sense no rebuke for their sin. What does the Scripture say? When a life is what God wants it to be, there will be an awesome and open blessing of God. I have often wept before the Lord and said, "Lord, I'm a sinner at best, and You will have to work through my life until I'm at least somewhere near where You want me to be. I will know I am there if You begin to implement openly in the midst of God's people what You said You would."

I've talked to many pastors who describe the lukewarmness of their churches. I ask, "How long have you been there?" "Seven years." I say, "They are the product of your walk with God. If you have been with a people for seven years, the Holy Spirit should absolutely come over them because the holiness of God is in your own heart. When you get up to speak, there ought to be this holy awe that demonstrates you have been in the presence of God." We *say* we are in the presence of God, but everything that God promises *will happen* if we are in the presence of God.

It is time for us to say, "It's me, O Lord." We should say, "O God, I will not rest, I cannot rest at night unless I know this servant is what You want him to be. I will know it as I walk among Your people and experience an obvious encounter with You that cannot be explained away because there is the awesome presence of God."

Do you hold yourself accountable as a servant of God? Do you look at the Scripture and say, "God says this is what should come when a person walks with Him"? But do you tell the people, "I walk with God?" Yet would you be more honest if you said, "Whatever you see in Scripture will happen with a person that walks with God. Please excuse me, but none of this is happening in my life, though I am still God-called?"

I have said, "O God, I cannot do this. I will not stand to tell someone that I have a word from God if I do not. If I have not let that word come through my life, I will not speak."

I sensed this longing when I listened to those college students. If I could gather up all the brokenness and sin that has been confessed, it would be a mountain. Then I said to the professors, "If these same young people can be in your classes week after week after week and still carry the utter brokenness of sin, there is something wrong with your teaching. These kids are weeping their hearts out. They would give anything if someone would have helped them get rid of this sin a year ago."

I looked at the pastors and said, "Do you recognize any of these students? These students attend our churches week after week. Their lives are full of sin, yet our preaching has no impact whatever. Something is wrong with our preaching."

When I was a pastor, I would grieve and say, "O Lord, if my people can listen to me on Sunday and still walk in sin, something is wrong with this preacher—not them, but me! What is missing in my life? What is it that God is not honoring?"

FROM THE HEAD TO THE HEART—JOEL 2:12-17

Let me put this passage in the midst of Scripture. The psalmist asks, "Who may stand in His holy place?" (Ps. 24:3). James 5:16 says it is the very active prayer of a righteous man that is powerful. I believe one of our greatest dangers is that we have it all in our head, but it is not in our heart. Do you know how you can tell if it has touched your heart? Jesus said it is spiritually impossible to have your heart in one condition and the fruit of your life in another. If we can say that we believe the things of the Word of God and say that they are in our heart but see no evidence of the implementing of those truths, then the Scripture has been in our head but has never hit our heart.

We have conditioned ourselves to think that, once we believe correctly and fill our heads with truth and thought, these truths are automatically implemented in our life. I ask many pastors, "Do you believe in prayer?" They say, "Absolutely." Then I ask, "Do you pray?" They reply, "Well, that has been the weak point in my life."

There is your problem: *You do not believe in prayer!* You do not believe in a God who issues a summons to come before Him. Has God ever summoned you into His holy presence? If so, did you come into His presence? Did you feel that God had transformed you with His Word? Did this so change your heart that you wondered what in the world had happened to you? That is when the truth from the mouth of God moves from your head to your heart. Jesus said what you see coming out of a person is indicative of that person's heart. We keep walking in the truth.

We say, "I believe in revival, I believe in awakening." But did you hear Joel 2:12-17? I do not know what you do about that Scripture, but I will tell you what I do. What did Joel tell the Levites? To wail, mourn, and grieve. That is a command! We have it in our head, but has it touched our heart? You will know when it hits your heart. You will cry with Jeremiah, "Oh, that . . . my eyes [were] a fountain of tears" (Jer. 9:1). But we can read the Book of Joel and never respond to the command of God. It is the spiritual leaders who must grieve. What do you do with this command? It is a prerequisite for God to withhold His hand of judgment. Do you believe if we do not follow that command the judgment of God will come?

PRAYER AND RESULTS—JAMES 5:16-19

We think God only wants us to say we believe something. But look at what follows: "Elijah was a man with a nature like ours, and he prayed earnestly that it would not rain; and it did not rain" (James 5:17).

What was the difference? He prayed. That is half the difference. But when he prayed, God *did* something. Have you been praying for revival? Many would say "Amen." Yet what evidence do you see that God has heard you? Does it concern you, when you read James 5:16-19, that nothing happens when you pray? Does America need revival? Has God put it on your heart to pray for revival? Has it ever gripped you? Does it bother you when you read this Scripture but nothing happens when you pray?

THE TEST OF FIRE—1 KINGS 18:36-37

Along with James 5:16-19, let us place 1 Kings 18:36-37. This could almost be a pattern for our praying as well:

It came to pass, at the time of the offering of the evening sacrifice, that Elijah the prophet came near and said, "Lord God of Abraham, Isaac, and Israel, let it be known this day that You are God in Israel, and I am Your servant, and that I have done all these things at Your word.

Hear me, O Lord, hear me, that this people may know that You are the Lord God, and that You have turned their hearts back to You again." (1 Kings 18:36-37)

Do you hold yourself accountable to that passage? Or do you say, "O God, at which point in this process am I grossly deficient? Is it that I have never heard you say, "let there be rain?" Is it because I am too far away to know what You are asking that I have had no word from You? Where in this picture have I not even come close to You?"

Can you examine James 5:16-19 and say, "Lord, would You make certain that I am righteous, that I have holiness as a pattern in my life, so that I can speak for You? Have You dealt with my life radically about sin and holiness? When I stand in Your holy place, are my ears open and my heart tender before You? Is sin there? Do my eyes understand what You are doing? Then I can go from that moment knowing there is a word from the Lord and that You will respond. Then the people will know that You are God and that at least one person is serving You and listening to Your Word." When you prayed like this, what was God's response?

John the Baptist preached: "Prepare the way of the Lord; make His paths straight."" (Luke 3:4). That highway is a Highway of Holiness. God uses a clean mind, a clean heart, and a pure heart. "Blessed are the pure in heart, for they shall see God" (Matt. 5:8). This is the kind of walk that God uses as a highway on which He will move mightily in revival.

I have been with many people who have prayed for revival with their lips but not in their hearts. God says, "You will know it is in your heart when you have met the criteria of holiness. Then I will start to move in mighty power in your life, your church, and out to the ends of the earth."

GOD'S DISCIPLINE—HEBREWS 12:7-13

God has a goal in mind when He chastens us: "That we may be partakers of His holiness" (v. 10). Verse 12 says, "Strengthen the hands which hang down, and the feeble knees"—symbolizing our prayer life. We must strengthen our prayer life.

I held my life up to this passage when I came to Howard Payne. I said, "O God, when I speak to the students, will You deal with my life so that the students will 'not be dislocated, but rather be healed'?" (v. 13). I prayed the students would be healed and not hindered in their walk with God. Then, I looked to see if any of the students were being healed.

Some of the students were trying to describe what had taken place while they were on the platform. One student said, "I... I don't know how to describe it. I've been healed!" I said, "My brother, you were! You were healed!" In my heart, I said, "O Lord, would You discipline me enough so that I can be a partaker of Your holiness, so that a highway to God is there when the spiritually lame are present and the Word is shared? May they go over that highway and come out healed on the inside."

If nobody is being healed because of our preaching, the problem is not the Word of God. The problem is not those who need to be healed. The problem is us. The tragedy is that God has so many of us in place, but there is so little healing in the lives of His people. There is no brokenness over that! We have said, "It's the day in which we live." We put the blame everywhere else! Revival comes from the leaders!

As when He called Elijah, God calls us and says, "I will shape you until you have a message to give. When you walk with Me and give that message, I will hold Myself accountable and do what you say. Then, they will know that I am God and that you are My servant and that you have done everything you have done because you are My servant."

When was the last time God demonstrated that clearly to the people where you serve? If you have to tell your people to follow you, you are in trouble. Is no one following you? Do you have to claim your authority as the pastor of the church? They will follow you when God puts it in their heart to follow you—when God can trust your leadership and when God has a leader like Elijah!

Does the holiness of God overwhelm you? Do you find yourself trembling when God speaks? The other day, I turned in the Word. When I read it, a trembling came over my life from top to bottom. I found myself spontaneously weeping. I said, "O God! Suddenly You have made me aware of how holy You are and how sinful I am. How much is at stake when I handle the sacred things! When I take this book, how much of eternity hangs in the balance! When I speak with people, how much You have in Your heart! Lord, I am totally unworthy of that! O God, if this is true, never let me speak again in Your name! Your holiness and my sinfulness are far apart!"

I lay there with no strength. I said, "O God, how could I possibly speak?" He said, "I will do in you what I did in Isaiah. He had no right to speak. I took coals and put them on his lips. You will know when I have done that." Then I said, "O Lord,
Hold me accountable for holiness. Lord, do not let me merely talk about it. Do not let me just read about it. You say it is the Highway of Holiness that will bring the people back to You. The people will rejoice, and they will sing."

Holiness is the highway over which God brings revival. Without holiness, no one shall see the Lord. No one can stand in His place without clean hands and a clean heart. The pure in heart will see God. May the Spirit of God teach us to pray, "O God, help me to see You," but only when we also pray, "O God, give me the conditions of heart that are prerequisite to seeing You. I cannot ask You to do a work in me unless I also ask You to do a work in my heart and in my mind and in my will." Without the prerequisite, this prayer is absolute foolishness. God will not send revival. Why have we cried unto the Lord and seen so little? Could God be waiting for His servants to walk over the Highway of Holiness? The unclean will not walk on it. Others will— those whom the Lord has ransomed and redeemed from sin, and dressed in His righteousness, now free in heart and mind before Him.

If, in some measure, any Scripture has been used of God to quicken our hearts and our consciences, we are talking about revival—about the survival of a nation, about the eternal destiny of others. We are talking about the honor of our Lord, about His name, and about being His servants.

Would you pray, "O Lord, begin this process. Do whatever You need to do in me?" Do not pray lightly, but with an understanding now from His Word.

May God grant us a quickened heart so that we will seek His holiness. If the Spirit of God brings to your mind anything that must be removed, ask God to deal with you with all of your heart and for His sake.

PART TWO
DISPERSION

Jonathan Edwards observed that the Spirit of God uses the sharing of testimonies of revival to spread the movement to other places. The following offers a summary of the dispersion of revival flames across Texas, to Wheaton College and other schools, and across the nation in colleges and local churches.

CHAPTER 7
THE SOUTHWESTERN STORY

MALCOLM MCDOW

Students of Christian history read about spiritual awakenings. Entire towns were spiritually purified, Christian lives transformed, churches energized, college campuses set ablaze, and the lost evangelized. Many ask, "Can we have revival today?" And many are praying, "Lord, do it again!"

That is what God did at Southwestern Baptist Theological Seminary, Fort Worth, Texas. Many students and some faculty members were touched with fire from the Holy Spirit.

PREPARATION FOR REVIVAL

Revival came when conditions were ripe for a spiritual renewal at the seminary. The school experienced turbulence after the dismissal of the president in the spring of 1994. This resulted in criticism, strife, suspicion, discontentment, bitterness, and confusion within the seminary family. This action intensified the prayer efforts of the administration, faculty, students, and friends of the seminary. Denominational controversy within the Southern Baptist Convention had affected faculty and students. Indeed, the heart cry of some faculty members and certain students was that God would divinely intervene and exercise His sovereignty. God answered those prayers on March 1, 1995.

God used many events to lay the foundations for revival. Southwestern's new president at the time, Ken Hemphill, led out in the preparation. His heart for evangelism and his emphasis upon lives committed to Jesus Christ provided the model and intensified the atmosphere for revival. His inspirational sermons in chapel, his exemplary Christian life, his pastoral compassion, and his efforts toward reconciliation were examples for the seminary family.

In August 1994, Hemphill mailed a letter to seminary alumni requesting prayer for the seminary. More than 1,500 promised to pray. T. W. Hunt preached a series of sermons on prayer in chapel during the fall semester. Calvin Miller preached the school's annual fall revival services.

Several groups of students had been praying for months for revival. Indeed, a few members of the faculty and student body had been praying for years.

FROM HOWARD PAYNE TO SOUTHWESTERN

After revival emerged at Coggin Avenue Baptist Church, Brownwood, Texas, President Hemphill invited John Avant to share the revival story in chapel. Professor Roy Fish wrote a letter inviting churches in the Dallas-Fort Worth metroplex to attend the chapel service on March 1. Fish wrote, "When the fire is falling, get as near as you can to the flame!"

A few students from Howard Payne came on February 28 to share about the Howard Payne campus revival in several seminary classes. As a result of these visits, many more seminary students formed prayer groups and began praying for revival. There was an air of expectancy. When you expect a visit from the King, you make sure you are ready for His visit. Southwestern was ripe for His royal arrival.

On March 1, 1995, the 1,200-seat auditorium was full. Others lined the walls, sat in the aisles, and stood outside in the foyer. John Avant shared the story of the revival going on in his church. He explained the background in his own life, conditions within his church, and the need for revival. He spoke of lives transformed, marriages reunited, and lost persons won to Christ. Many felt a strong sense of the presence of God. It was a spiritual excitement before the storm. There were no emotional outbursts and no overt audible demonstrations. Instead, many sensed a holy hush hovering over the congregation. Avant spoke for about forty minutes. He gave no formal invitation but stated that he wanted to allow the Holy Spirit to do whatever He was pleased to do. It was about 10:50 A.M.

Several students and faculty members moved to the front of the auditorium, formed groups of two and three, and knelt in prayer. No one left the room.

HONEST CONFESSION

After two or three minutes, one student moved to the microphone and shared what God had just done in his life. Suddenly, students filed one after the other to the microphone to share. Many praised God for His glorious grace and wonderful love, mercy, forgiveness, long-suffering, and kindness. Many confessed secrets of their souls and experienced cleansing, forgiveness, and reconciliation with God and with others.

As the service progressed, people left the campus only if necessary. Many classes were dismissed. Word spread across campus that something unusual was occurring in the auditorium. One professor shared with the listeners that he had gone to the cafeteria and found it empty. Some students stepped outside, called long distance to their home churches, shared the event and requested prayer.

Testimonies continued without pause until after 4:00 P.M. Even then, many lingered in the auditorium, huddled in small prayer groups, or prayed alone. Prayer groups remained in the auditorium until after 10:00 P.M. Revival had come to many lives.

"FORGIVE MY PREJUDICE!"

One student shared that he had been reared in a family that harbored racial bias; and consequently, he was a racist himself. He testified that God had worked in his life, convicting him of his racial prejudice. As he directed his remarks to the black students in the congregation, he asked that they forgive him. As he left the microphone, two African-American students met him. They embraced and knelt in prayer. That Anglo student and one of the black students became prayer partners.

Another student shared that she had some attitudes toward some professors that had created barriers in her relationship with God. The student asked each professor to forgive her for these attitudes. As the student returned to her seat, one of the named professors embraced her in the aisle. In the midst of the chapel service, a trustee shared with the congregation. A verbal confrontation followed between the trustee and a faculty member. Some worried that it might hinder the revival. One student who was standing behind Avant on the platform said, "Oh, God, don't let them kill it." Shortly after the verbal exchange, the professor got into the confessional line and shared that, whatever his feelings were about the trustee action, his sin was bitterness. He asked for forgiveness for quenching the Spirit. He turned to President Hemphill and told him he loved him and would stand with him. It was a wonderful moment. The students applauded. We could sense healing had begun to take place.

As unchristian habits were confessed, one student shared the habit of using snuff, testified as to what God had done in his life, placed the box on the pulpit, and said, "No more." Student after student revealed inner conditions of lust, use of questionable literature, and watching less-than-wholesome movies as they confessed sins that formed walls between them and God.

LIVES REFOCUSED

Scores, literally scores, confessed and testified. A student confessed dishonesty on tests and shared that he was going to each professor and make restitution. Another student confessed that he had misused telephone codes at work. He shared later that when he told his supervisor, he was dismissed from his job. However, he expressed gratitude to God for His work of grace. Later he testified to his church, "I don't have my job, but I have my integrity."

Other students shared how they had lost their focus in ministry. "I have been so busy doing God's work," said one student, "that I have not been doing God's will. I came to the seminary to prepare for the ministry, but I neglected my walk with Jesus. I thank God that He has not forsaken me. Today, I have my life refocused."

"Several years ago," testified a young wife, "I lost my mother to cancer. I was so mad at God for taking my mother that I told God that I would never go to church again. For some reason, God led me to marry a preacher, and we came to the seminary. What do I know! Even so, I have lived in rebellion against God. I have lived in fear. God has taken away my rebellion this morning. I don't fear anymore. God has taken these away! Thank You, Lord."

"I thought I was a Christian. Last fall, I had surgery," testified one student. "In this experience, I sensed that I did not have the kind of relationship with God that I needed. I have struggled with this for several months. God has answered my prayers. He has come into my life today and has given me the assurance that I am saved."

"WHY HAVE I COME HERE?"

One student shared, "I have asked myself, 'Why have I come here? What is this all about?' I want to be pleasing to God. But I have been going about it wrong. It has been what I have wanted to do and the way that I have wanted to do it. God is teaching me that it is not my way that matters, but His way."

"I have been struggling to obey God," shared a young man. "God is teaching me that obedience leads to death, for Paul said in Galatians 2:20, 'I am crucified with Christ.' It is this walk with Christ that I so strongly desire. God has been teaching me that I have been living my life all wrong. I have been doing it my way. God is making it known to me today that I am to love and seek Him, and He will take care of the rest. It is as if the world has been lifted from my shoulders."

Still another student shared, "I needed to wake up! God knows I needed to wake up! I have gone to sleep on Him. I have been teaching a Sunday school class and attending seminary classes, but I have not been having that quiet time with Him. He has convicted me of my neglect. Lord, how I needed to wake up!"

"My parents are not Christians. My life has plateaued. I have had no burden for my family," said a young man. "Imagine! My parents could have gone to a Christless hell, and I might have never told them how to be saved. God, forgive me. I promise God right now that I will tell my parents about Jesus. Pray with me that they will be saved."

Yet another said, "For several months, I have prayed for something like this to happen. I have prayed and confessed my sins. Yet there was one thing lacking—my actions! They were still the same. God has convicted me that my actions must agree with my confessions. Thank You, Lord, for being merciful."

PRAY! PRAY! PRAY!"

In the middle of the testimonies, Dr. Jack Gray, retired professor of missions and a consistent prayer intercessor for revival moved to the microphone and exhorted the hearers to be open to the Holy Spirit and be obedient to God. In closing his appeal, he spoke in almost inaudible words as he whispered softly and compassionately, "Pray! Pray! Pray!" Although those words were whispered, they resounded throughout the auditorium like roaring claps of thunder as they fell upon human ears; and many did pray and pray and pray.

While some students prayed at the altar, others testified at the microphone. One single student shared, "I have been trying to make some decisions about school. My family is opposed to my being in the seminary. I don't have a very good relationship with my parents.

Because of this, my relationship with God is not very good. God has convicted me this morning. I am going to get things right with my parents. I knew all along that God is the answer, but I was not willing to turn it all over to Him. I thank God for touching my life and getting my head on straight again."

One student confessed, "I knew that I was going to heaven, but I was not burdened about others. God has convicted me that I need to serve God today, live in His will today, be burdened for people today, witness to people today."

There was another student that testified, "For several months, I have been praying that God would do something in my life that would make Him more special to me than He has ever been before. I had the idea that it could take months to do it. God does not need a year, month, week, or even a day. God is doing it now."

Still another student shared, "I have been out of fellowship with God. I have been reminded today by God that we don't suddenly decide to get away from God. We do it one sin at a time. He has convicted me that I am not walking with Him. God, forgive me! Forgive me! If you have not come to grips with our Holy God, I beg you to open your life and let God have freedom to work in your life right now."

IS THIS GOD'S WORK?

For five and a half hours students confessed immorality, spiritual negligence, and bitterness. In response to the chapel service, many offered evaluations of the unusual spiritual movement. It has been compared with the Asbury revival in February 1970, and the renewal at Southwestern on March 16-19, 1970. Avant summarized the experience when he said, "God is shaking us—something no person can do."

Michael Dean, pastor of Travis Avenue Baptist Church, Fort Worth, Texas, said, "The service was a refreshing movement of the Lord. I genuinely sensed the presence of the Holy Spirit. It is a confirmation for me that God wants to do something great in Fort Worth."

Ken Hemphill said, "I, for one, experienced a genuine touch of the Holy Spirit, and He is continuing to do a work in my life. A genuine touch of the Spirit will bring humility, not arrogance."

Hemphill firmly stressed, "Revival will intensify your hunger for the Word of God and for prayer. It will be evidenced in your lifestyle, language, witness, joy, and discipline. It should produce a great zeal 'to study to show ourselves approved unto God, workmen that need not be ashamed.'"

Roy Fish said, "I have no question that what happened was of God. I am hearing about a new freedom on the part of many people who were touched by God."

AFTERGLOW

When revival comes, what then? Any genuine awakening will have lingering impact. As one seminary professor said, the confessions in chapel "will move them to service. To be genuinely of God, the emotions of the chapel service March 1 have got to be moved to Christian service that benefits the church." Another professor noted that the Christians in the Book of Acts did not stay in the Upper Room, but the Holy Spirit thrust them into the world to plant churches and evangelize.

What about the afterglow at Southwestern? Was it simply an emotional chapel service that was only temporary with no lingering impact? Did this spiritual renewal really impact ministries? The testimonies of many students reveal that indeed there have been ongoing effects. One student shared, "I did not experience revival in the service. It was not until I got back to my room that God got hold of me and turned me every way but loose. Oh, that experience with God! I will never forget it. I know that my life is changed forever."

A student pastor reflected upon the service and the impact upon his life. "Last Wednesday, I attended the chapel service prayerfully expecting God to do something. He did not disappoint me. As I reflect back on the events of that morning, I remember words from the chapel service, 'Revival is for believers, and we choose whether or not to participate.' That morning I asked God to show me my sin and help me be the leader He intends me to be. My sin was pride, and God showed me the kind of pride He opposes. I looked down my pious nose at the less-educated gentry and refused to be tamed. As my acquaintances tried to warn me of my illness, I never understood what they were saying; the change was so subtle that I did not feel sick. Last Wednesday, God loved me enough to refuse to let me go until the pain of my sin hurt me more than ignoring it. For that, I praise Jesus Christ who refuses to let go of those He loves. The cynics can wait until they can securely judge the repentance of their siblings, or they can entertain the possibility that they, too, are infected with ivory-towered academic pride."

One student shared, "A lot of people at Southwestern have realized that the holiness of God has been lacking. God is reminding us that His holiness is more than morality. It is being set apart from the world."

The ultimate effects of the revival will be reserved for God to determine. Many lives that were touched by the Holy Spirit have entire ministries in order to produce the fruit of the renewal. The immediate results can be seen in changed attitudes on the parts of many—different atmosphere, sins forgiven, purging, cleansing, and refocused directions for living. The long-range results will be weighed on the scales of eternity and determined within the mind of God.

THE NEWS SPREADS

Before the day was over, the media was alerted and came to the campus. Reports of the revival appeared on the evening news. Calls began to come from across the United States inquiring about what was going on.

As the news of the revival spread, the media from around the nation called for interviews. A Christian radio station in Atlanta, Georgia, carried a thirty-minute interview with Avant and McDow. The Moody Broadcasting Network, with 180 radio stations nationwide, devoted a ninety-minute program to the renewal at Wheaton, Houston Baptist, Howard Payne, Beeson, and Southwestern. Other religious publications and secular newspapers carried the story.

The revival on March 1 came at a perfect time for Southwestern. For more than thirty-five years the seminary has sent student revival preachers to churches across the United States, Canada, and other foreign countries during spring break. There were 95 preachers who went to 103 churches to preach in revival meetings during the week of March 12-19. In some of those emphases, renewals occurred.

One student went to a church in Iowa. The church had

an attendance of only fifteen to twenty, but five of those were youth. God began to move in the lives of those five. They began to talk to their friends at school. About seventy young people attended the Friday night service. Spontaneously, the decision was made to rent the high school gym, which was located across the street from the church, and have an overnight youth lock-in. Some of those teenagers were converted. The seminary student shared, "I had reservations about going. I really didn't know why I was even going. Now I know why."

Another student went to Colorado. He shared that God moved powerfully. During one service, many stood, testified, and confessed that their relationships were not right with God; but with God's help they were committing their lives anew to Him. That church was touched by God.

Yet another student went to California. At the beginning of the week, a man began visiting the services. As he sat on the back row each night, he listened intently to the messages. He came under deep conviction. Toward the end of the week, he made a commitment to Christ. As he talked with the young evangelist from Southwestern, he handed two bullets to the student. In explanation, he said, "I am a veteran of Vietnam. What I experienced in that war has messed up my life. I have carried two bullets with me for all of these years. One was for me when I could not go on living any longer. The other was for anyone who tried to stop me. I don't need them any more. Jesus has changed my life. I have something worth living for."

REVIVAL IN OUR TIME

We can proceed in living as usual, relying on traditions,

customs, personal agendas, and our own desires. However, these are destined to falter and fall. When we live within our own resources, we plateau and decline. We lose the joy of service, celebration in worship, and victory in living. No Christian can live on the capital of past experiences even if they are experiences with God.

Can we have revival today, or is revival something only from the past? The revival at Southwestern has taught us that revival in the then-and-there are merely affirmations that revival most assuredly is for the here-and-now.

CHAPTER 8
JERSEY VILLAGE BAPTIST CHURCH

ALVIN L REID

"God-organized chaos." This is how one person described the most powerful service I had seen in a local church as an adult. It reminded me of when I first met Christ during the Jesus Movement in 1970.

In January 1995, God began a fresh work in my life. I had to make some changes. I would have missed the activity of God had I not listened to Him in January. My problem was busyness, which represents a key symptom of my struggle with pride. I was always in a hurry because I thought my schedule was more important than anything else. Then, I cut some things out of my calendar and made my family the priority they should be. That gave me time to listen to God throughout the day—what a novel thought!

REVIVAL SPREADS TO HOUSTON

Many members of the Jersey Village Baptist Church in northwest Houston had gone through *Experiencing God* and *Fresh Encounter.* Several believers had begun praying on Monday nights for spiritual awakening. Attendance increased from four hundred to eight hundred in a fairly short span.

While the church was completing a new worship center, the church had three worship services every Sunday. Because of this exhausting schedule, the pastor asked me to preach there on four consecutive Sunday nights in February.

The service was packed on the night of February 5. A great spirit permeated the place with several decisions but nothing extraordinary. The next weekend a *Disciple Now* was held among the church's youth. Sunday night, February 12, many youth testified that God was working in a fresh way. The service lasted two hours.

A RISING TIDE OF THE SPIRIT

The next week I attended the National Convocation on Revival in Little Rock. John Avant and I embraced in tears, not speaking a word, for what seemed like five minutes. We prayed for years to see what God was now doing. It's one thing to pray for years and quite another to experience the fruit of those prayers! The next Sunday, I shared the Brownwood story with Jersey Village. John sent Howard Payne students Brandi Maguire and Kelly Parrish to come there Sunday night, February 26.

On Sunday morning, February 26, God began to move. No sermon was preached. People shared testimonies, prayed, and experienced God's presence. Some deacons had gotten their own hearts right with God the weekend prior in a deacon retreat led by Pastor Rodney Woo of Wilcrest Baptist Church. 1 had been up at 2:00 that morning, compelled to pray for the services.

Kelly and Brandi shared in the evening service. Brandi said, "Walking into these doors and experiencing what I feel here tonight is exactly what is happening at Brownwood." That statement almost knocked me out of the pew.

After Kelly and Brandi spoke, I told the church: "When Brandi said what she did, it really amazed me. In 1970, students from Asbury College in Kentucky came to

Fort Worth to share with seminary students. One Asbury student said, 'You don't need us. You are experiencing exactly what we are.' That is what Brandi just said!"

Brandi's testimony confirmed the genuineness of the Spirit's movement at Jersey Village. I told the congregation, "Revival is never corporate until it is first personal. In the Welsh Revival of 1904-5 Evan Roberts gave four principles for personal revival: (1) confess every known sin, (2) lay aside every doubtful habit, (3) obey the Holy Spirit promptly (4) confess Jesus publicly."

After giving these, I opened the floor for testimonies, confessions, or for anyone to share a burden on the heart. So many people shared that the service lasted almost four hours.

One woman began weeping, confessing anger and confusion. "I've got a war going on inside me," she said. Several ladies began to pray with her.

I was concerned that such open, profusive expressions of emotion would alarm some who had never seen anything like this in a church service. "I've been in a service many times when people shared spontaneously," I said. "If you have never been in a service like that, it may be uncomfortable for you. We don't want it to be. When there is fire, there is always the danger of wildfire. But, sometimes we miss the real, Holy Spirit fire because we fear wildfire. So you pray for those of us in leadership."

A man stood and read Scripture. Another older man stood and exclaimed, "I was taught Christianity is going to church; I was not taught it is a relationship." He shared his deep burden that people truly encounter God personally. A teenager told about his struggle to have a pure heart and mind and about his concern over his relationship with his brother, who had run away from home. People of all ages shared.

PERSONAL STRUGGLES

I then let the pastor take over the leadership of the service. Many came to the altar to confess or testify. When one person finished, a group would gather around that individual for ministry and prayer. Then another came to share.

One woman was distressed that her unbelieving husband opposed her church attendance. Several women with unbelieving husbands ministered to her. A man stood and testified that for years he had harassed his wife for her faith until God broke him and saved him. A high school student confessed his struggle with the lust of the flesh. He asked for help to control his lust and to be an effective witness for Christ. Many high school students gathered around him for encouragement.

A teenager came forward, sharing how her father had been a pastor and was treated wrongly by his church. She asked the church to pray for her father to find a pastorate. People flooded around her at the altar to pray. Many youth came, confessing sin, broken with concern for family and friends, and seeking a fresh walk with God.

There were three microphones on the stage. When one person finished sharing hurts, people would gather all around the person to minister to them. These groups became so numerous at the altar that the pastor was surrounded. At times he had to lay the microphone down on the floor and go to another microphone to continue.

A high school student came forward to confess sin. At first he was unable to speak because he was in such agony. Men gathered around him and prayed for him. After a few minutes he was able to confess that he had such a vile mouth at school that he could not be a witness for Christ.

One boy, probably ten years old, began to weep as he told the congregation of his burden for his lost grandfather. Others shared similar concerns for lost friends and gathered in groups to pray

"I'M PREGNANT"

I wept when a fifteen-year-old girl told the congregation, "I'm pregnant, I'm scared, and I need help." Again, people flooded around her to pray and offer support. What a glorious picture of the body of Christ restoring one who confessed her sin and her need! The pastor told the people, "Our church must be a church where young people can come when they have erred, be loved, and be ministered to in Christ."

While this pregnant girl was receiving ministry, a mother took a microphone and told the congregation that she also had once been pregnant out of wedlock. She had to decide whether to have an abortion and kill her baby. Her thirteen-year-old daughter was seated in the pew, sobbing uncontrollably, as she hugged her mothers' neck. The daughter realized her mother had spared her life. The mother told how that daughter was the joy of her life. What a ministry God did for that scared young girl facing an unexpected pregnancy!

Another young woman came to the microphone. She once had a child out of wedlock. Today she is married. She told how her young child was such a great joy to her. Again, God mercifully ministered to the young pregnant girl. [Note: see the follow-up to her story in Chapter 14]

A FAMILY RESTORED

Another of the most moving events involved a rebellious young man, the one whose brother had requested prayer for him earlier. He had left home two months earlier because of his bitter relationship with his parents and was staying with other church members. The evening of February 26, the young man's mother and father were working in the preschool area. One of the other two sons was present that night and was asking the church to pray that his disobedient brother would be there that night, though he knew that was humanly impossible. His brother was in Galveston partying at the Mardi Gras festival that very day.

About that time the Minister of Students asked that someone relieve the workers in the preschool area. They had been working more than two hours, and he wanted them to participate in the service. As the preschool workers were replaced, they joined the congregation, including the mother and father of this prodigal son.

The mother went to the microphone to ask for prayer. She confessed that there was a separation in their family because of their son. Meanwhile, the son had come back from Galveston to the house where he was staying, but no one was at home. It was well past the time for the family to be home from church; so he went to the church looking for them, still wearing Mardi Gras beads around his neck.

As he came through the back door of the church, his brother could not believe his eyes. His mother was sharing her heart with the church, not knowing that the disobedient son had come in. As she was speaking, the pastor saw the son in the back of the church. He called out for some of the men to bring the wayward son to his mother, saying, "Bring the boy home! The prodigal has come home!" I will never forget the sense of God's power I felt as this young man walked forward. About seven men stood and walked with him. The prodigal *had* returned!

His mother had difficulty in embracing him because of the bitterness between them. Women gathered around her and prayed for their reconciliation. Then, in tears she hugged her son.

His father was on one knee praying. The son came, knelt, and put his head on his father's knee. His father tried to put his hand on his son's head, but could not because of the dissension between them. Men gathered around them, prayed for them, and ministered to them. They said, "Just love your son." The father then was able to put his hand on his son's head. It was a beautiful scene of reconciliation as they embraced. God had restored fellowship and brought a wayward son home. Amazing grace from God!

A teenaged girl asked the pastor, "How can I be a part of this?" She was paired with a woman to go and hear about salvation in Christ. After about twenty minutes, she came back and it was announced that she had trusted Jesus as her Lord and Savior. As this young girl saw God's love permeating a group of people and could see clearly the disciples of Jesus loving one another, she desired that love also.

After about four hours, the service closed with great joy. People joined hands and sang "Sweet, Sweet Spirit" and "Blessed Assurance." The congregation clapped almost five minutes in complete joy and praise for God.

REVIVAL CONTINUES

At eight o'clock the next morning, a woman came to the church to work out a severe problem. Four women (including the pastor's wife) went to the church, ministered to her, and prayed with her for two hours. Phil Woodruff, a member at Jersey Village, was so moved by what he witnessed on February 26 that he wrote an eight-page letter to family and friends describing the activity of God. He commented: "I stand in amazement at what my eyes have seen and ears have heard take place last Sunday." He closed his account by signing his letter "an eyewitness to God's glory."

On the next Sunday a man felt a need to talk to someone in a church. He opened the phone book and saw Jersey Village Baptist Church. He called the church office. The minister to children led him to Christ over the phone. The man said he was coming to church that night, and he did. What he did not tell her was that he had no car. He *walked* more than five miles to get to the church service!

Other incidents occurred which demonstrate a spirit of revival continued. Individuals continued to be reconciled to one another. Prayers were answered in marvelous ways.

SARAH'S STORY

On the night of February 26, a teenage girl told the congregation about her burden for her nine-year-old sister, Sarah. In tears she spoke of her sister's Down's Syndrome condition which caused the older sister to wonder if Sarah could understand how to be saved. God answered her prayers. Here is a letter from Pris Baughn, a member of Houston's First Baptist Church and a special needs teacher at the local public school where

Sarah attends:

The week before Easter something happened that made me want to give your church body a special "pat on the back." Our Life Skills students at Post Elementary were preparing to dye eggs for their Easter egg hunt. One of my co-teachers asked the students to tell one thing that they think of when they hear the word *Easter.* There was silence for a few minutes and then one little hand went up.

Sarah Bales stood to her feet and began explaining that Easter was about Jesus dying on the cross with a crown of thorns on His head. At the teacher's request Sarah sat down to give other students a chance to tell what they knew about Easter. When there were no other answers, Sarah again raised her hand and said, "That's not all. Jesus is *alive,* not dead! He died for our sins and He *arose* up to heaven where He lives!" The teacher complimented her for her nice answer and then asked her to give other students a chance to answer. Again there was no response, and Sarah spoke up to say, "There is one more really important thing that I wanted to say. Jesus died for our sins and we can ask Him into our heart." Sarah ended by saying, "That's what I learned in my church last Sunday and then when I got in my car my mommy and daddy talked to me all the way home."

Needless to say, we were left speechless, until one little boy turned to Sarah and said, "If you can ask Jesus into your heart, I can too." Sarah's reply was, "Everyone can, silly. Everyone knows that."

I still can't believe what I heard from the heart

of a nine-year-old child with Down's Syndrome.
Sincerely,
Pris Baughn

Revival can touch the heart of a wayward son and bring him home; release the forgiveness of God to a teenager who has erred; deepen the relationship between God and His children who formerly walked in legalism alone; and open the heart of a mentally challenged young girl to the truth of salvation.

CHAPTER 9
REVIVAL AT CORINTH, TEXAS

DOUG MUNTON

It was the week following an incredible Sunday night service, one that had lasted for more than four hours. Dozens of people had made public confessions of sins and requests for specific prayer. I was trying to analyze what had happened. Had it been genuine revival or just a temporary emotional binge? Would there be any lasting results or was it just a momentary shot in the arm? Then people began to tell me about what God was doing in their lives.

One woman told what had happened to her family. They had said nothing that March 4 Sunday night service. They had left before it was over because a neighbor's child they brought needed to go home. Later that night, she and her husband prayed for each other and for their spiritual needs. This was the first time they had ever prayed aloud together like that in their lives.

Other couples would later tell similar stories. Several told me they had gained a burden for witnessing. People began to report that they were sharing their faith with their friends and especially with lost family members. Soon we began to see the fruit of their labors.

A SEARCH THAT RESTORES

One young adult had shared nothing publicly the night of the confessions, but later said he felt a burden to renew a broken relationship. Fourteen years earlier his father had left the family in a painful divorce. For a long time this young man felt bitter toward his father. He had since forgiven him, but he had not spoken to his father for those fourteen years. On Monday after our incredible service, the young man began to search for his father.

He eventually traced his dad who had moved a few times and was living in South Texas. He told his father that he had forgiven him for leaving the family and that he wanted to restore their relationship. A few weeks later, the young man saw his dad for the first time in fourteen years and introduced him to his daughter-in-law and three grandchildren. He also shared his faith with his dad and is praying that he soon will have the privilege of introducing his father to Jesus Christ as his Lord and Savior.

HEARTCRY FOR REVIVAL

I have had an interest in revival for a long time. As a student I wrote my Ph.D. dissertation on J. Edwin Orr, the historian of spiritual awakenings. I have often talked about revival with John Avant, Alvin Reid, and other classmates. We wondered if we would ever see God move like He did in those great revivals.

As a pastor I have yearned to see a real movement of God in my church. I have prayed for revival and preached on revival. I have even seen a few touches of revival. During my first ten years at First Baptist Corinth, we had tremendous growth. There have been some wonderful spiritual harvests. Lives have been changed, believers strengthened, and discipleship deepened. But I always wondered if we would ever see real revival sweep our church family.

On March 4, 1995, our church began to experience a

genuine time of revival. That is not to say that everyone in our church family was revived; nor does it suggest that we have suddenly become everything we should be. But something began that evening that has made a tremendous impact on many people and has had lasting results. I believe several things led up to this moving of God.

LAYING THE FOUNDATION

One precursor to revival was a fresh emphasis on discipleship. Since 1992 more than a hundred of our adults have completed *Experiencing God* by Henry Blackaby and Claude King. It was life changing for many of us. Other small group discipleship programs have started. Many have taken the courses *Disciple's Prayer Life* by T. W. Hunt, Promise Keepers for men, and courses on parenting and marriage enrichment. These courses emphasize fellowship and spiritual growth to our church family. More than sixty of our men attended the Promise Keepers rally in Dallas. Many were deeply stirred by the event.

Early in 1995, I began expecting God to do something special at Corinth. My devotional times got stronger. I began to sense renewed vision for our ministry, something that had been lacking for a while. But it was also a difficult time at our church.

THE NEED FOR REVIVAL

Before I came to Corinth, First Baptist had been declining. On my first Sunday, we had only nineteen in Sunday school. Our church grew consistently for eight years, but then our growth rate began to slow.

The 1994 church year was hard for me. In 1993 we grew 25 percent but in 1994 only 10 percent. That was the slowest growth rate in my ten years as pastor. Many good things were occurring; but several factors hindered, including tremendous space problems. We were growing and baptizing a good number of people, but I had grown frustrated. Then early in 1995 God started to renew my spirit. Once again I began to believe that God was going to do something special in Corinth.

THE FIRES FALL

John Avant began to tell me about happenings in Brownwood. This was the first I had heard of a campus awakening since the 1970 Asbury Revival. I listened and prayed with growing excitement.

I asked John to send us some Howard Payne students to share what God was doing. We scheduled them to speak on Sunday evening, March 4. John continued to update me about what God was doing, and I passed this along to our church family. Anticipation mounted. We had an evangelistic campaign scheduled for the week before the students were to come. A great deal of preparation for that meeting was done. Evangelist Frank Harber began our evangelistic campaign on Sunday, February 26. He preached well. But the meeting was going along in less than dramatic fashion — that is, until Wednesday, March 1. That morning we went to Southwestern Seminary to hear John Avant speak in chapel.

When I walked into the chapel, I felt God's presence. I said to Frank, "I feel a revival spirit!" That was the first time I had ever said anything of that sort. Even today it is hard to explain that feeling. There was a holy hush among those in the room. Many students were in prayer. I felt a tremendous urge to pray, and I did for the next several minutes.

Frank and I ate a late lunch that day with John Avant and Professor Malcolm McDow. We gloried in what God was doing. I was deeply moved and told these friends what I would be confessing to my church family.

That same Wednesday evening was Youth Night in our evangelistic campaign. Frank preached a powerful message. Twenty-seven youth made professions of faith and many others recommitted their lives to Christ.

The following Sunday night the Howard Payne students came to share. I expected two or three students, but a van showed up with seven. Three Southwestern students came because they heard the HPU students were coming.

THE PASTOR CONFESSES

My testimony came first. During the Southwestern chapel, I felt that God wanted me to make a public confession to my church. I told my church about how we had grown so well for so many years and how that growth had slowed in the last year. I said there were several reasons for that slowdown. One was obviously our terrible lack of space. Our adult Bible Study classes had to meet in a nearby elementary school with air and heat that sometimes did not work. "But," I said, "that is not the only reason for the slowdown of our growth."

I confessed, "I have not been what God wanted me to be as a pastor. Several pastor search committees have spoken to me about being their pastor in the past year. I had allowed this attention to distract me from what God wanted to do in Corinth. I began thinking, *what if God moves me somewhere else?* I have stopped calling you to step out in faith. I have allowed my vision to be clouded."

Part of my sin was based in pride that made me think God owed me "a more significant ministry." That pride kept me from appreciating the tremendous privilege God had given me to be able to preach the gospel at all. Later I came to realize that part of the problem was my fear of failure and lack of faith. I feared that our church would plateau and sink into complacency. I lacked faith that God could use someone like me. Maybe I should abandon ship before things started getting bad!

I have since discovered that many pastors share these same problems. We swing back and forth. One side is pride in our own abilities and accomplishments, as though we don't need God. On the other side are our insecurities and fears of failing, as though God won't be able to use us. The two sins seem distant, yet they are so commonly discovered in the same person.

I confessed all this to our church family, then prayed with them and recommitted myself as their pastor. It was a moving time for us as a church family. I was the only pastor many of them had ever had. It was moving for me as well.

Several students from Howard Payne and Southwestern shared what God was doing in their lives and at their schools. They told of how God was helping them to grow spiritually, how they had been convicted of sins, and how relationships were being restored.

After about thirty minutes of sharing, I asked our congregation to spend some time in prayer. Then I said, "If anyone has something they need to confess or something to share, the microphone is open." For the next several hours our people began to confess their sins and ask for prayer for their needs.

THE PASTOR'S WIFE CONFESSES

My wife, Vicki, was the first to confess. She shared how she had allowed her feelings of low self-esteem to become an excuse for not witnessing and not allowing God to do things through her instead of trying to accomplish things for Him in her own strength. She asked for prayer that she would not allow past difficulties to keep her from doing what God wants her to do.

After Vicki spoke, many others came to the microphone. Many leaders of our church family made confessions early in the evening. Others followed, including many who rarely came to a Sunday evening service. Often I found myself surprised when people came forward, first because they were in attendance, and second because they were going to say something in front of everyone else!

FAMILIES RESTORED

One college student stood and in tears confessed that he often had a rebellious attitude toward his mother (who was in attendance). He apologized to her publicly and declared his love for her. He said, "I have heard people say that how you treat your mother is how you will treat your wife. Right now, I don't recommend any woman marrying me!"

Others came to confess bitterness, rebelliousness, or strife with other family members. Several older children confessed disobedience to their parents.

Two teenage girls confessed that they had not been getting along with their older brothers as they should. They spoke of their deep desires to have a close relationship with their brothers.

One touching moment came when a father of two children confessed his lack of consistent, godly parenting. Through his tears, he said he longed to be a godly example to his little boy, like his father had been for him. He asked the congregation to pray that he would not lose focus on this most important task in his life.

APATHY CONFESSED

Several stood to confess their lack of service to God and His kingdom. One noted that I had taken some of the blame for the slowdown of growth in our church. He confessed that he shared the blame as well due to his lack of service in the church family. Others noted that they had never been willing to allow God to use their gifts and abilities for His glory in the church. They committed themselves to God's work in the future.

One man stood to say that he had sometimes told people that our church is unfriendly. He had been coming to the church for a few years and only knew a handful of people. The problem, he now confessed, was with him, not the church. He confessed that he had been unfriendly and asked our prayers and support as he committed himself to opening up to others and being sensitive, and therefore vulnerable, to them.

One of the beautiful things that happened that night was the support people received from others. People who spoke were soon surrounded by others who would pray with them. It was a moving scene that was repeated over and over. Finally, after four and a half hours the service closed.

THE REVIVAL GOES ON

People were so excited about the service they hated for it to end. I believed, however, that the revival was far from over.

God moved powerfully again the next Sunday evening, March 11. The crowd was larger than usual. I sensed it was going to be a great service. I thought there would probably be several people who would want to confess sin. When I came to the pulpit, I read my Scripture text from Isaiah 55. I called the people to prayer and again opened the microphones to anyone who wanted to speak. To my surprise, no one came! After a few minutes I went back to the pulpit and preached the message I had prepared.

As I preached a message on revival, I sensed God's presence and the audience was unusually attentive. During the invitation several came to pray. One man asked if he could share a confession of sin. After the invitation time was over, he shared how he had missed opportunities to witness that week and asked that we would pray that he would boldly share his faith when those opportunities came.

EVIDENCE OF REPENTANCE

Then a most surprising thing happened. A longtime church member came with a trembling voice to tell me privately that she had been praying and fasting all day about something. She has been one of our hardest workers. She had been out of town the previous Sunday night, but she had been praying ever since that the revival would continue. During her prayers that day she asked God to reveal anything in her life that might be hindering revival. What she believed God showed her, and what she needed to do in response, was unusual.

She said that she had always struggled with authority figures. She believed God was convicting her of her need for a servant heart and a submissive spirit. She asked if she could wash my feet as a sign of her submission to me as her pastor. I said something like, "What!?" That made me feel uncomfortable, but I felt that she was sincere and that it was from the Lord. I agreed to allow her to wash my feet.

She then confessed to the congregation her improper spirit. She said, "I like to be the boss, and it's hard for me to be a servant." She told the congregation of the permission she had received to wash my feet as a sign that she wanted to serve her church and her God. Then, as others continued to confess sins at the microphone, she began to wash my feet with a wet towel. Her husband knelt and tearfully joined her. It was a moving experience and powerfully illustrated to our congregation God's desire for a servant's heart among His followers.

PUTTING FAITH INTO ACTION

Specific confessions of sin and requests for prayer continued for two hours. Many admitted their lack of evangelistic activity and requested prayer for individuals they knew God wanted them to witness to. There seemed to be a greater emphasis on putting the Christian faith into practice. Several voiced concerns about family members who were lost.

The next several weeks saw a continuation of the revival spirit. People continued to share what was on their hearts, sometimes through confessions of sin, sometimes through testimonies. New freedom and openness characterized the church family, particularly in the Sunday evening services.

Early in the revival time I asked advice of several

people. Malcolm McDow suggested that I preach on revival and encourage those who had been cleansed and renewed to move into practical service to God. I preached through Isaiah, explaining how to put revival into practice. Many who had experienced personal revival became involved in ministry and evangelism.

In a few weeks many people came to Christ, including several adults. One man had been coming to our church for several years. Somehow, he came with some regularity for those years without trusting Christ as his Savior. Many of us had witnessed to him repeatedly. He was, I am certain, the most prayed-for man in our church! When he finally made public his profession of faith, the church family could not help but burst into applause at God's goodness.

A LIFE TRANSFORMED

Mike came forward in our March 4 service to confess that he had been on the sidelines in his spiritual life. He had been baptized in our church several years earlier, but he had not taken any responsibilities or active role in ministry. A rather quiet young man, he asked the congregation to forgive him for his spiritual apathy and lack of transparency. He later said that the March 4 service was "the most life-changing experience in my entire life."

Not long afterward, Mike became burdened for his family members. He asked me to pray with him for his mother who was not a Christian. Later, Mike told me of the results of his witness encounter. He became very nervous as he contemplated talking to his mom. He said he started to speak with her several times but "chickened out." Finally, after earnest prayer, he asked his mother for permission to share the plan of salvation with her. To his delight, she agreed.

Mike's mother has not yet accepted Christ, but she promised to go to worship and Bible Study each Sunday morning for three months. She has been coming faithfully now for the past month. On a recent Sunday morning, Mike asked if he could share the story of his witness to his mother that night. He wanted us to join him in prayer for her and to be encouraged by his witness. Naturally, I was delighted for him to tell the story. What we didn't know was that Mike's sister would be in attendance that evening, which was probably her first-ever Sunday night service. She had begun to attend the morning services with her mother, and Mike was unsure of his sister's relationship with God.

During the service Mike told the story of his witness to his mom. As the service progressed, he noticed that his sister was crying. He began to talk with her and discovered that she had never trusted Christ as her Savior. In their seats, as the service continued around them, Mike had the privilege of leading his sister to faith in Jesus Christ.

BEARING FRUIT THAT REMAINS

God's work in our church family is far from complete. Many have yet to allow God to bring revival to their hearts. The spiritual work is only beginning. But it has been encouraging to see the renewed emphasis on holiness, discipleship, and evangelism that has occurred in Corinth. We believe the revival will bear fruit in changed lives for years to come. I have had the privilege of sharing the story of this revival in other places and have seen God use it to spark the stirring of awakening.

I close with this disclaimer. I did not lead the revival. Only God can lead revival. My role has been in three areas.

1. I had to get my life right with God. Continued disobedience or apathy among church leaders hinders the coming of revival.

2. I had to get out of the way. When God wants to work, I serve God best by allowing people to confess and testify without trying to stifle or control. I attempted to use discernment, but when God was leading people to speak I found it best for me to stay out of the way. Our nature is to program and direct. Revival is not a program.

3. I encouraged people to move into practical service. Emotion and forgiveness must not be the end of revival. We must put into practice healthy habits and consistent service. I have tried to facilitate the renewed desire people have to serve.

Perhaps there is one other role. It could be that through the telling of the story of revival, others will be challenged and renewed by God. I pray that the telling of this story of revival in one local church will help in some small way to fan the flames of revival across our nation and throughout our world to the glory of God!

CHAPTER 10
THE MOVEMENT FROM TEXAS TO THE NATION

DOUG MUNTON AND DAN R. CRAWFORD

A Los Angeles weather forecaster said concerning southern California fog, "If the fog is going to lift today, it will take a wind from somewhere else."

In the winter of 1995, Brownwood, Texas, and Howard Payne University experienced a "Wind from somewhere else." Like the Wind in Acts 2:2, it "filled" the place where believers gathered and then moved on from Brownwood and beyond those whom He touched.

This is an account of some of the places where this fresh wind blew in the weeks and months following the Brownwood experience. Indeed, "The wind blows where He wishes" (John 3:8).

REVIVAL'S SPREAD ACROSS TEXAS

HOUSTON BAPTIST UNIVERSITY

On Tuesday, March 14, Tim Williams and Richard Robeson shared with students at Houston Baptist University. Professor Alvin Reid arranged for them to share during the activities period at 10:00 A.M. Reid said, "When you hear that revival has broken loose, you either go where it is or bring it where you are."

The Fellowship of Christian Athletes on campus hosted the meeting. News traveled by word of mouth. About sixty students, faculty, staff, and four or five local church staff members gathered. Howard Payne students shared their testimony during the activity period. Then, those who gathered moved into prayer groups. About twenty stayed for a time of confession, prayer, and testimony that lasted until after 1:00 P.M.

Senior Jason Seifert, a student leader, shared his burden for a Christlike love for all students, regardless of race. He recounted an incident in which he had driven a van to a Baptist Student Union function. He drove the van that carried all of the African-American students. They had a great time; but for some reason, when the group stopped to eat, the Anglo students ate with Anglos, Asians with Asians, and blacks with blacks. Jason shared how he longed to see God bring students together.

Students shared their lack of burden for lost students, and many talked about a need for accountability. Each time one shared, another would lift that individual up in prayer.

The movement at Houston Baptist grew, as seen in the Thursday night campus student worship called QUEST. The Howard Payne students shared at QUEST on March 16. The group who gathered numbered well above the average and the largest crowd in some time. Beginning about 8:45, the service lasted until midnight. Again, the time was marked by testimonies, confession, and reconciliation.

The university student newspaper, *The Collegian,* featured an article the following week entitled "Revival Brings Students Back to First Love." Writer Jessica Wallis reported: "Last week Christian students at HBU joined for worship, prayer, and open confession during two campus meetings." Senior Jason Seifert compared the time with similar events at Howard Payne: "We confessed that we haven't upheld the two greatest commandments of God: to love Him with all our heart, soul, mind, and strength, and to love our neighbors as ourselves." Freshman Jeremy Jansen observed, "Individuals are becoming more spiritually aware, and I think corporate revival has to start like that."

Senior David House testified to a personal change out of the QUEST service. "I was convicted of sin in my life, my attitude, and my outlook. I truly realized I still had sin in my life and needed to confess that to my Christian brothers and sisters. It was odd that I even attended QUEST, because I wasn't planning to go." Other students said they also experienced God moving in their lives at QUEST.

The following week at QUEST no special service was planned; however, students who gathered stayed until 11:00 P.M., confessing, worshiping, and praying together. On March 30, one week later, professor Reid invited John Avant to speak to students at that night's QUEST. About two hundred students gathered for the service, a remarkable number for the mostly commuter school. After telling the Brownwood story, Avant opened the floor for testimonies. Many students shared. Prominent leaders confessed addiction to pornography. Others shared struggles with problems ranging from eating disorders to alcohol and drug use.

A recent graduate shared that God had recently set him free from his addiction to pornography. His professors, friends, and even his family were at the QUEST that night. After he shared, his father shared how he was sorry for his example before his children because his own addiction to pornography had influenced all of his sons. Some young ladies confessed their hidden bulimic or anorexic life styles and sought help.

The *Houston Chronicle* featured a story on the revival and this service in particular. In the article entitled, "Baptist Revival Phenomenon Surging," writer Richard Vara reported, "Houston Southern Baptist Churches are among churches and schools reporting a wave of spiritual revival reminiscent of the 'Great Awakenings' in American history." Vara, who attended that service at HBU, commented on the prevalence of open confession of sin as a characteristic of the movement.

UNIVERSITY OF TEXAS AT ARLINGTON

Baptist Student Union and Chi Alpha (the Assemblies of God campus ministry) sponsored a two-night tent revival at the University of Texas at Arlington, April 17 and 18. Christian leaders at UTA were seriously interested in revival. The campus had been torn by controversies among administrators, faculty, and students.

I (Doug) was asked to come and speak about revival. The leadership also contacted some students from Howard Payne University. Only about fifty showed up for the first night of the meeting. The wind, gusting to nearly fifty miles per hour, was whipping the sides of the tent in a noisy percussion. There were many distractions during the service. Students listened politely, but it was not the breakthrough we desired. I left after the first evening thinking revival would not come to this secular campus.

The second night was different. The weather was beautiful. The sides of the tent were removed, and there was a much more open feeling. The crowd doubled. I spoke from Isaiah 6 on revival. Concluding my message, I asked people to pray.

After a few moments, a girl came to the microphone and confessed that she had gotten so busy with school, work, and even religion that she had not taken time for God. She shared in a sweet, humble way her desire for intimacy with God. For the next hour students continued to come to the microphone to confess sins. Some gave testimonies of God's victories in their lives, including a student who told of being delivered from homosexuality and another who told of his recent conversion from the Islamic faith to Christ. Many confessed broken relationships and bitterness towards others.

THE CRISWELL COLLEGE, DALLAS

At the 1995 Day of Prayer service on March 23 at Criswell College, two students from Howard Payne and I spoke. Jay Jones shared, as he had at my church and other places. The students and faculty who were present listened with rapt attention. After sharing, the Howard Payne students began to pray.

I told about the Corinth revival and about what God had been doing in my life. After reading a portion of Isaiah 55, 1 urged students to surrender their lives fully to the Lord. I opened the microphones up to those who needed to confess.

After a minute, a student came to the microphone weeping. He confessed that he had gotten so busy that he had ignored his relationship with the Lord. After speaking for a few moments, he went to the altar and began to pray. Fellow students surrounded him and began to pray with him.

Students confessed and prayed for several hours. One young man confessed that he had falsified a reading report. He had just confessed this to the professor and now asked forgiveness from his classmates. Others made similar confessions.

A young man stood to confess some property he had stolen. He had been active in the First Baptist Church of Dallas, the church that founded the school. Some time earlier, a pastor of the church had resigned and some bitter feelings had resulted. A portrait of the pastor had hung in a prominent place in the church. After the resignation, the portrait had mysteriously disappeared. The disappearance had been the source of much speculation. This young man confessed that he had taken the painting, and arrangements were made to return the portrait to the church.

Other schools in Texas have reported touches of revival. Some students were moved at Hardin Simmons in Abilene and at Wayland Baptist University at Plainview. At First Baptist Church, Lubbock, students in the college department had times of extended confession and repentance in late March. Certainly many other college students were influenced by stirrings of revival on campuses and in local churches.

CHURCHES IN THE HOUSTON AREA

Alvin Reid invited Howard Payne students Tim Williams and Richard Robeson to visit Houston on their spring break, March 13-17. They first visited the area headquarters of the Fellowship of Christian Athletes, where a scheduled one-hour session quickly became over five. There was confession, praying, singing, weeping, and sharing.

That night the two young men spoke at revival services for the First Baptist Church of South Houston. According to Pastor Hughes, "What followed can only be described as a movement of God. People began to come forward and confess their sins to one another: lust, bitterness, anger, hatred, a lack of compassion, a lack of commitment, alcohol addiction, etc. The response of the congregation was fantastic. As people came forward to confess, others came forward to minister. It was truly the body healing the body." A man in his seventies testified that he had been a member of that church for forty-five years and had never seen God move like He did that night.

During March, Reid led a seminar on spiritual awakening for four Wednesdays at the Baybrook Baptist Church in Friendswood. He decided to scrap his seminar and let the people hear of the current activity of God. Tim Williams shared his testimony there on March 15. Several members shared their burdens for revival and some particular concerns. The following Wednesday night a lengthy time of brokenness, confession, and ministry continued for more than two hours at Baybrook.

Tim shared at Wilcrest Baptist Church on March 19. During the previous week, Pastor Rodney Woo had called the church to prayer. Most of the morning service was given to deep prayer for revival. On April 2, the youth Sunday school department didn't make it to the worship service on time. Woo finally found out why. The youth were on their faces in prayer from 9:30 to 12:30.

During these same days, a similar outpour came during First Baptist West Houston's annual retreat. Deacon Jeffrey Russell explains: "We saw Him establish His unmistakable foothold in our midst. Morning turned rapidly to afternoon, as many decided both publicly and privately that Jesus Christ had been for too long a 'distant cousin.' God was at work. The next several weeks prompted a cascade of evidence of God's character. Unusual conversions, powerful testimonies of changed lives! God surpassed our prediction of His ways. On a Sunday night, many confessed and testified openly. Rarely had the Holy Spirit touched our church like this. God continues to work."

Pastor Larry Kindrick testified about the First Baptist Church of Atascocita. On March 5, 1995, Jerry Wiles from Houston Baptist University shared about the revival which had broken out in Coggin Avenue Baptist Church and its spread. God's Spirit visited in a unique way. There were tears of repentance and joy. On Sunday night the Holy Spirit took over as a large number of people came forward and filled the altar to pray for healing and spiritual renewal. One person said, "I've never been in a service where I felt the presence of God so heavily."

On March 31, more than fifty pastors from a diversity of denomination shared an extended time of confession after hearing John Avant share about Brownwood.

On Good Friday, April 14, Houston's First Baptist Church held a Solemn Assembly, which featured Brandi Maguire's testimony. The assembly lasted six hours— more than one and a half hours were given to confession of sin.

CHURCHES IN THE DALLAS/FORT WORTH AREA

Birchman Baptist and Sagamore Hill Baptist reported revival coming out of services with Life Action Ministries, as well as special services with John Avant. Southcliff, Travis Avenue, Southwayside, and other churches had powerful services after the March 1 awakening at Southwestern Seminary.

Rodney Woo preached revival services for the Connell Baptist Church, Fort Worth, April 9-12. On Tuesday night, people began to share and confess sin. Woo described what happened.

> Something unbelievable happened. A member stood and confessed she had been instrumental in forcing the termination of the last pastor. She had met with the personnel committee and deacons, talked to anyone who would listen to her, and worked to rid the church of this pastor. She told the church she would be calling the former pastor that night to seek his forgiveness. Then she said what she had done had been a part of a corporate sin of the entire church.

> I did not know exactly what to do. I pled with God to give me wisdom. I then reminded the people that, just as we commit personal sins, we also can sin as a body. I then asked anyone else involved in the former pastor's forced termination to come to the altar to pray as a body. More than one-half of the congregation came forward. I led them in a joint confession, walking through Psalm 51. Many people age sixty and older asked the church to forgive them of pride, bitterness, insensitivity, lukewarmness, and divisiveness.

Revival has come to many other Texas churches. Certainly there is a great need for others to join in the spirit of brokenness and confession. Revive Your work, Oh Lord!

THE MOVEMENT ACROSS AMERICA

As noted in earlier chapters, the spirit of revival spread to various places including the context of previously scheduled events. These included the North American Convocation on Revival in Little Rock on February 14-17, 1995, and the Spring Evangelism Practicum at Southwestern Seminary where students spread cross the nation during spring break to speak in churches.

Revival began to spread among the college and university campuses of America. Like Howard Payne students, Wheaton students began to share their experiences in churches and on other campuses. One such church was in Sioux City, Iowa, where three students spoke. According to the pastor's wife, a graduate of Wheaton College, entire families, including small children, exhibited, "great brokenness, love, and compassion."

COLLEGE CAMPUSES AWAKEN

A flood of repentance during services at Colorado Christian University mirrored similar activities that were on other campuses. Here, twenty-five students who had planned to drop out of school decided to stay. According to University Chaplain, Woody Northcutt, "What happened in the last two weeks has changed their lives, and they want to come back and see more of what God is doing."

Christian students at Iowa State University in Ames, Iowa, experienced similar responses on April 10, when approximately three hundred members of several Christian organizations on campus waited for several hours to come to the microphone to confess sin, repent, and pray. Beginning at 8:30 P.M. with testimonies from four Wheaton students, the meeting lasted until 5:00 A.M. Mike Sutton, Campus Crusade for Christ Director, said,

"I sat there stunned. The effects of sin on Christians' lives were so prevalent."

Spiritual renewal first emerged at Liberty University, Lynchburg, Virginia, during the Spiritual Emphasis week, September 11-14, 1994, when Randy Hogue shared with the faculty and students. Great evangelistic results followed. Hundreds of students made professions of faith, renewed commitments to Christ, and experienced deep conviction of sin and meaningful healing. On January 29-February 1, 1995, the school had the second Spiritual Emphasis Week with evangelist Rodney Gage as speaker. God moved in a powerful way in the lives of hundreds of students. On Wednesday, February 1, the microphone was offered to anyone who felt led of God to speak. For three hours, continuous lines of people formed to testify and confess. God moved among the audience of fifteen hundred and brought genuine brokenness of sin.

On April 9-10, 1995, more than two hundred students gathered for prayer in the chapel and on the lawns of the campus. For eleven hours, they prayed as the Holy Spirit worked in lives.

The revival wind continued to blow across campuses: reports of revival experiences came from Indiana Wesleyan College, Marion, Indiana; Bethel College, Mishawaka, Indiana; Judson College, Elgin, Illinois; George Fox College, Newberg, Oregon; Multnomah Bible College, Portland, Oregon; Louisiana Tech University, Ruston, Louisiana; Illinois Baptist College, Galesburg, Illinois; Crown College, St. Bonifacius, Minnesota; Messiah College, Grantham, Pennsylvania; Geneva College, Beaver Falls, Pennsylvania; Spring Arbor College, Spring Arbor, Michigan; Biola

University, Los Angeles, California; Cornerstone College, Grand Rapids, Michigan; Criswell College, Dallas, Texas; Texas Southern University, Houston, Texas; and the University of Georgia, Athens, Georgia.

THEOLOGICAL SCHOOLS

Beeson Divinity School of Samford University in Birmingham, Alabama, witnessed a touch of God's Spirit following a message by John Avant.

When it was announced at Southern Baptist Seminary in Louisville, Kentucky, that John Avant was preaching in chapel, there was a rumored student boycott of the service. The students saw Avant's scheduling as an administration ploy to divert attention from the problems of the school.

Thom Rainer, dean of the School of Missions, Evangelism, and Church Growth (and currently president of Lifeway Christian Resources) and Avant's host, shared his concerns with Avant. They decided not to cancel classes, which would probably eliminate an invitation. Also, there would be no open microphone for confession. These and other decisions came from a desire to avoid any appearance of emotional manipulation.

A small crowd was anticipated because of the boycott, but approximately one thousand students attended. One man said later he had driven six hundred miles to be there because he knew that "God was up to something great!"

After Avant spoke, students were dismissed for class. But hundreds stayed. Although no microphones had been set up for confession, Rainer looked up at one point to see a line of students on the stage. Avant looked to him for direction, and Rainer looked to the president, Al Mohler; but Mohler was on the floor praying with a weeping student. Rainer and Dean of Students Doug Walker gave the "go ahead" to Avant. Rainer said, "I am glad that we let God have His way!" Students confessed sin for a lengthy time.

Some confessed bitterness, anger, and resentment. "It was a very spiritual and emotional time," said a student from Maryland. "It dug deep and brought out a lot of feelings I had been hiding a long time."

Rainer reflected on the day: The fruit of their changed lives is increasingly evident in more fervent prayers, in restoration of relationships, in greater hunger for God's Word, and in zeal for the lost. I believe they can never again be satisfied with status quo Christianity."

A similar revival came at Trinity Evangelical Divinity School in Deerfield, Illinois, April 3-6. A statement from the school listed characteristics of the movement including confession, repentance, prayer, spontaneity, minimal structure, reconciliation, and restitution.

Church history professor John Woodbridge said of the revival, "I have never seen anything quite like it in twenty-five years of teaching here."

CHURCHES AND CONFERENCES

The Illinois Baptist State Evangelism Conference meeting in O'Fallon, Illinois, on Wednesday, March 15, saw an extended session of public confession and repentance following a retelling of the Brownwood, Texas, and Southwestern Baptist Seminary experiences. Immediately following the recounting, people lined up at the podium to confess sins, ask forgiveness, and pray. Many came to the altar to weep and pray. Others formed small prayer groups in other parts of the auditorium.

The pastor of a church that started nearly twenty-five years ago when members split from another church said God had convicted him that the two churches needed reconciliation to erase longstanding bitterness. He was joined at the podium by members of the other church who prayed with him. Nearly five hours into the session, many were still standing around the altar; and many others were praying.

Gerald Stefly, director of missions for the Metro Peoria Baptist Association, said, "Young people, old people, black people, white people, all kinds of people responded. The confession and prayer time lasted two hours. The service went past eleven o'clock. It was an awesome sight as we saw God move in a mighty way. Words are inadequate to express what God did, what our hearts felt, what our eyes did see, and how our hearts long for God to work in our own areas."

As a direct result of the Illinois Evangelism Conference, Pastor Nathan Argent shared the story with his First Baptist Church in Carlyle, Illinois. He described the church prior to March 19 as "in desperate need of renewal and revival. There was a lot of discouragement." Following the Evangelism Conference sharing, ninety people were in attendance on Sunday, March 19. Of the ninety, thirty came forward to confess and pray. Similar experiences happened in Southern Baptist churches all over Illinois as pastors shared the O'Fallon experience and church members responded in confession, repentance, and reconciliation.

One Illinois director of missions was so touched by

the Evangelism Conference experience that he returned home and played excerpts of the tapes at his weekly pastors' meeting. The pastors canceled their afternoon appointments in order to remain and pray. Central City Baptist Church in Centralia, Illinois, was in a revival meeting that week. Pastor Ron Bracy began the service that night sharing the experiences of earlier that day and then confessed his own sins before the people. Evangelist Frank Harber never got to preach that night as the people began to stand and confess sins and pray for each other. The service lasted for three hours and gave impetus to a genuine sense of revival in the church. About thirty persons were saved during the meeting.

CHURCHES COME ALIVE

Pastor Jim Henry, president of the Southern Baptist Convention, challenged the First Baptist Church of Orlando, Florida, on March 5 to sixty days of prayer and fasting for their non-Christian friends leading up to their revival meeting in May. According to Evangelism Pastor Bill Mitchell, 257 members pledged to fast one meal per week, and 437 other members promised to fast one day per week. But God didn't wait for May. On Palm Sunday, April 9, Pastor Henry stood to preach. Instead, he told the congregation he felt led to have the choir sing and let God lead. Almost immediately several people responded. One prominent church member stood to apologize to the congregation for not being faithful to the church. This was followed by other confessions and exhortations.

The invitation time lasted more than an hour with thirty-five to forty conversions. No sermon was ever preached. The Palm Sunday service was telecast on Easter, and nine more persons called in to profess faith in

Christ. During the Easter dramatic presentation, more than three thousand people witnessed eight performances of "The Light: The Story of Our Christ" with 927 persons inviting Christ into their lives. When the revival meeting finally came, another fifty-eight professions of faith were recorded.

SPRINGDALE, ARKANSAS

On March 28, 1995, Ronnie Floyd, pastor of the 9,000-member First Baptist Church of Springdale, Arkansas and current president of the Southern Baptist Convention, felt convicted he should fast for forty days. He began on April 15 and fasted until May 25. During these days, Floyd committed himself to pray that revival would come to himself, to his church, and to America.

On May 30, he wrote a letter to the entire membership, asking the church to convene on Sunday, June 4, with every mind focused on revival. On June 4, Floyd preached on revival and offered an unconventional invitation. He said, "Revival is the manifest presence of God. Right now we want to be still and let God speak."

For more than an hour, confession, brokenness, and restitution marked the service. Floyd says, "It was the greatest spiritual movement of my ministry. We closed the service with the announcement that the evening service would resume where the morning service left off. More than two-thirds of the congregation returned for the evening service. We started at 6:30 P.M. and went past 10 P.M.

"From time to time throughout the service, I shared that anyone who needed to leave could do so. But nobody seemed to want to leave. When a person confessed a particular sin, that person would kneel at the altar while others who had similar problems knelt with the person. I asked those who had experienced victory over that problem to go to the people and render ministry. For more than three hours, the service was a spiritual powerhouse." Similar morning and evening services continued the following Sunday.

On Thursday, June 8, fifty teenagers fasted and prayed for youth camp, June 12—17. The camp turned into a time of revival. More than thirty youth were converted. Confession of sin and reconciliation among youth characterized the week. One young person said, "Everybody was changed."

Even on July 2, a holiday weekend, crowds overflowed the 3,500-seat auditorium to celebrate the theme "Revive Us, O Lord." The service became another experience of the mighty movement of God's Spirit. Sins were confessed, including pride, lust, drugs, drinking, and failure to tithe. Floyd says, "The best word to express what God is doing is *incredible.*"

Although members of the Elkhorn Baptist Church in Campbellsville, Kentucky, had prayed for revival, they were unprepared for God's response for their revival services beginning March 26. So great was the response that the meeting was extended from six to twelve days and moved to the auditorium of South Campbellsville Baptist Church, which seats 750.

Other churches joined in, and even the larger auditorium overflowed. Elkhorn pastor, Dan Hunt, said he knew that "God was up to something" when he looked up from praying and saw he was surrounded by people on their knees at the altar. South Campbellsville pastor, Brian Fannin, said, "It was as though one could feel the wind of the Spirit blowing. It just seems that for a moment God opened up the windows of heaven and allowed us to glimpse what He can do." As revival moved forth, Elkhorn's secretary, Karen McMahan, said, "Everywhere I went—to the grocery, the convenience store, wherever—people were talking about the revival."

The local ministerial group called a day of prayer and fasting for Campbellsville. Hunt recognized that God sovereignly moves in revival but also noted how He had prepared Elkhorn for this movement. After 175 members of the church went through *Experiencing God,* they hungered to join God in His activity.

INDEPENDENT REVIVAL MOVEMENTS

Olivet Nazarene College in Kankakee, Illinois, reported experiences similar to those elsewhere but without any apparent connection with events at Brownwood. Student Matthew Horn gives this report:

> Thursday, February 23, we headed into chapel like normal. Nobody knew what was going to happen. We were preparing ourselves for the campus winter revival services, which were to take place the next week. So, this Thursday Chaplain Bray began to talk about what revival is. He started by telling of the great revival that started at Asbury College back in 1970 that spread through many college campuses at that time, fueling a fire that swept across the country. While he was talking, a student walked on stage and stood next to him. That was highly unusual and something that made everyone take a breath wondering what was going on.
>
> Dr. Bray stepped aside and allowed the student

to speak. What came out of his mouth was truly something that the Holy Spirit wanted him to say. He spoke about the prayers that were going on for this revival, and that something special had happened in his life because of these prayers. Then a staff member walked up and started talking about what the Lord was doing in his life, and how he was released from anger and frustration. Then a second student took the stage, and a third, and a fourth, and a fifth. Each one testifying to the wonderful power of the Lord!

One of my friends on campus got up and said that this looked a lot like crowds at Woodstock, but this wasn't exactly like that; it should be called "Godstock."

Chapel that day lasted more than seven hours. On Sunday at the College Church of the Nazarene, there was electricity in the air. People lined up spontaneously to share. As Horn put it, "It was Thursday all over again, and it was really great."

The Asbury story from 1970 also sparked revival among students at two Kentucky universities. At Morehead State University, a group of students watched *When God Comes,* a video about the 1970 Asbury Revival. Students remained for an extra two hours to pray, confess sins, and sing. Baptist Student Union Director Gene Parr says, "The soil is ready, and when God speaks, the seed is ready to grow." Across the state at Murray State University, 130 students attended the showing of the video. Keith Inman reported a strong response including many fresh commitments to Christ and several professions of faith.

During the biennial meeting of the staff of the

Campus Crusade for Christ at Fort Collins, Colorado, in July 1995, revival ignited among the participants. More than four thousand United States staff members plus many international workers heard Nancy Leigh De Moss of Life Action Ministries speak on Monday morning of the conference. Spontaneously, the Holy Spirit worked the process of conviction in the lives of the people. The service on that Monday lasted until after midnight. For two days and more than eighteen hours, the people confessed, shared and received cleansing. Staff members had come to the meeting with expectation of God's movement, and they were not disappointed as God worked powerfully in the conference.

In North Carolina, a college student named J.D. Greear and his friends had begun a Bible study that met on Monday nights at Campbell University. The group grew to between 100-200 by his senior year in 1995. This led to J.D. and his friend Bruce Ashford—both of whom are leaders in the church today—to start an awakening-focused ministry to college students.

Indeed, "the wind blows where He wishes" (John 3:8), and these are only examples of where and how God's revival wind has blown in recent days. May these accounts spawn revival in our time.

CHAPTER 11
REVIVAL AT WHEATON COLLEGE

TIMOTHY K. BEOUGHER

World Christian Fellowship (WCF) is a student-initiated, student-led gathering with a focus on world missions. It meets regularly every Sunday evening at 7:30 P.M. in Pierce Chapel on the campus of Wheaton College. Normally attended by about 450 students, more than twice that number gathered on the evening of March 19 to hear testimonies from two Howard Payne University students about a movement of God on their campus. After a brief welcome and the singing of two choruses, those present raised their voices in song with the following prayer:

Let Your glory fall in this room
Let it flow forth from here to the nations
Let Your fragrance rest in this place
As we gather to seek Your face.

World Christian Fellowship meetings normally end by 9:00 P.M., but that meeting went on until 6:00 A.M.! These meetings continued Monday through Thursday, beginning at 9:30 P.M. and lasting until about 2:00 A.M. This chapter is an overview of this remarkable week in the life of Wheaton College

PRECURSORS TO REVIVAL

Matthew Henry observed, "When God intends a blessing for His people, He sets them a praying." People around the world have been praying for revival at Wheaton College.

In the fall of 1994, I saw several indications that God was burdening people's hearts to pray. Following a challenging chapel message in October, one student organized a twenty-four-hour prayer chain to pray for revival at the college. Students signed up and participated for several weeks. Numerous groups with a focus on prayer were forming all over campus. November 9 was designated as an all-campus day of prayer, with many in the college community participating in special opportunities for prayer throughout the day. Two hundred students came to the first prayer time—at 5:30 A.M.!

In addition to prayer, attention was focused on the phenomenon of revival through a booklet written by Mary Dorsett entitled "Revival at Wheaton." Complimentary copies of this publication were distributed to the campus community. In addition, courses which studied the phenomenon of revival were offered in the spring of 1995 by Lyle Dorsett ("Evangelism and Renewal"), Kathryn Long, ("Revivalism"), and a course that I teach entitled "History and Theology of Revival."

I attended the North American Convocation on Revival held in North Little Rock, Arkansas, from February 14-17 where Henry Blackaby and John Avant shared about the revival on the campus of Howard Payne University. I came back to Wheaton and reported to my History and Theology of Revival class what was taking place.

On March 2, I shared what I had heard about the revival the day before at Southwestern Baptist

Theological Seminary. I pointed out the connection between what had taken place in Brownwood and the events on Southwestern's campus, emphasizing something we had studied during the course—a person who has been touched during an awakening is often used by God to carry the "spark" of revival to other places. We discussed the analogy of kindling: Prayer and preparation "stacks the kindling," but God often uses an outsider to bring the "spark" to light the fire.

With this in mind, I asked Matt Yarrington, a student in the course and the chairman of World Christian Fellowship, if WCF would be interested in inviting Howard Payne students to share how God had worked on their campus. Matt presented the idea to the WCF Cabinet. After much discussion, prayer, and consultation with Kevin Engel, assistant director of the Office of Christian Outreach and staff advisor for WCF, two Howard Payne students were invited to share at the WCF meeting on March 19.

SUNDAY, MARCH 19

There was an undeniable sense of anticipation in Pierce Chapel. Nate Fawcett, the leader of the worship team for that evening, opened the meeting at about 7:30 P.M. A few days earlier Nate had written the following memo to the WCF Cabinet:

The theme for tonight, as most of you probably already know, is "When God Moves." I am extremely excited, a little scared, in great anticipation, and a little tired, but I can't wait for the evening of the 19th. We will begin with a short overview of the evening to let people know where we will be headed, and specifically to allay any fears about the nature of the evening. We have no intention of trying to re-create a revival that happened somewhere else, no desire to "force" an emotional response from those present, and no specific way in which we want to see God move. What we do want is to be as open as possible, giving God free reign to work as He wills. God is sovereign and will work in His ways in His time, and nothing we do will force His hand one way or the other. As we listen to the two students from Texas, we want to foster an atmosphere of rejoicing for what God has done, and also an atmosphere of introspection—an opportunity to look at ourselves and ask God to meet us in a new way.

Nate highlighted the key themes of his memo, emphasizing both a caution—we are not trying to reproduce something that happened somewhere else—and a hope—we want to be open for God to move however He wants to in our midst.

Following a time of praise and worship, Brandi Maguire spoke first, opening her remarks by saying, "Nothing I could share with you tonight could give God the glory that He deserves." She talked about the movement of God's Spirit at Coggin Avenue Baptist Church on Sunday morning, January 22. She told the story of the Tuesday night meeting during the week of special services at Howard Payne and how God began a deep work in the lives of many students.

As Brandi shared, a "holy hush" began to permeate Pierce Chapel. College students can sometimes be a rather difficult audience, but she had everyone's undivided attention. She talked about how a group of junior high girls in Brownwood were fasting during their lunch hour to pray for their unsaved friends. Brandi paused and then asked, "When was the last time you skipped a meal to pray for a lost friend?"

She concluded by saying with deep emotion, "My heart is broken for you, that you will break your hearts before the Father, because He desires that." Then she sat down. I sensed that God had already begun a powerful work in our midst.

Jay Jones followed Brandi and did a beautiful job of telling what happened at Howard Payne University. I believe Jay's testimony was important in our context because he made it clear that he had become rather cynical about the prospects of revival at Howard Payne during his three and a half years there. He wasn't involved with others in praying for revival. He certainly wasn't anticipating the events that took place.

Jay talked about how God had done a deep work in his own life and how he had been humbled to the point where he publicly confessed his sin in front of fellow students. He said, "I went up [to confess] more scared of God's judgment than that of my peers." Three things stand out about what Jay shared. First, he emphasized his reluctance to accept what was happening on campus, and how God had impressed upon him, "Jay, I don't need *your permission,* I want your *submission"* Second, he cited Amos 7:7 and talked about God's plumb line. When God holds up His standard against our life, things we have deemed acceptable are suddenly seen as unacceptable. Third, he cited James 5:16 and asked why most of us had ignored that verse all our lives.

He closed in prayer, echoing the caution against manipulation but expressing his desire that all of us be open to what God wants us to do. When Jay finished, Matt Yarrington announced that two microphones would be available for student response. Matt said, "We are going to open it up right now for a time of questions, testimonies, confession of sin, or whatever the Lord leads you to talk about." He cited Charles Finney's definition of revival: "a new beginning of obedience to God." Matt said, "I need that—and I think we all do." He then prayed and sat down.

The first Wheaton student to share confessed anger and bitterness toward the campus because of a hurtful situation the year before. He said that God had shown him his need to forgive and be forgiven. A second student confessed sin in his life and asked for prayer and accountability from the college community. At that point, Kevin Engel took the microphone on the platform and led us in prayer for these two students.

As each moment passed, lines at the microphones grew until they wound halfway back the outside aisles of Pierce Chapel. Students, one after another, openly confessed sin in their lives: bitterness, lust, anger, jealousy, pride, cheating, racial prejudice, hatred, addictions of all kinds, theft, cynicism, materialism, competitiveness, broken relationships—you name it.

What took place as students continued to share was a beautiful picture of the body of Christ in action. After each confession, a group of five to twenty-five people would gather around the person and minister love, acceptance, and encouragement. There was a continual flow of people into and out of the auditorium all evening as people would leave to call friends or to go and bring them back to Pierce.

The time of confession, which began at

approximately 8:50 P.M., continued until 6:00 A.M., when it was decided to end this meeting and reconvene at 9:30 P.M. that night. For more than nine hours, scores of students had openly confessed their sins one to another.

THREE IMPRESSIONS

I recall three distinct thoughts that raced through my mind throughout the night as I sat and listened to the confessions.

First, I must admit I was a little nervous when the sharing began. I have studied spiritual awakenings for fifteen years, but I had never been in a meeting with this many people when the Spirit of God was working in this way. For one who likes the admonition "let all things be done decently and in order," it was a little unsettling for me. Perhaps part of my concern was generated by thoughts of a recent article I had written on the camp meetings of the early 1800s, where emotional excess was commonplace. I was literally sitting on the edge of my pew, prepared to jump up and "lead" if things seemed to get out of hand.

The Lord reminded me of a section in the course I teach titled "Leadership in Revival." My lecture notes, from which I had taught just a few weeks earlier, read as follows: "One of the reasons why we fear revival is that we can't control it. But that is the whole point—God is to control it! In real revival, God is in control—that is what makes it revival! We don't need to allow unwholesome extremes, but we must let God be God in revival and allow Him to direct it."

It was as if the Lord said to me, "As I recall you taught this to your students with great passion—you taught it like you really believed it! Well, you're the student now—I'm going to show you just how true those words are!"

For the next several hours, indeed for the next several days, I saw our sovereign God superintend His work in our midst. I mentally made a note to scratch out the large *L* in Leadership in that section of my notes, changing it to a small *l*. In genuine revival there is only one Leader—Almighty God.

Second, I was impressed that students were violating the principle of public confession that I had been taught to follow: "Let the circle of confession be only as large as the circle of offense." They were confessing private sins before several hundred people.

As I reflected upon this, several thoughts came to mind. Many students had confessed their "private" sin over and over to God but still found themselves in bondage; perhaps public confession is the starting point in breaking the stronghold that sin has in their life. The depth of pain evidenced by many who shared left me amazed that some of them had even been able to get out of bed that morning. I was struck that many of these students had become so isolated that they had no individual or group to whom they could be open and honest. That's why, when God convicted them of sin, it all came out.

I was discussing my mixed emotions a few days later with our chaplain, Stephen Kellough. He suggested that perhaps *the paradigm needs to be rephrased:* "Let the circle of confession be as big as the circle of offense—or as big as the circle of *solution.*" In other words, even though the wider community may not have been part of the "problem" or had any awareness of the sin, they became part of the solution in terms of prayer, encouragement, and accountability for the students who confessed.

My third impression was a deep awareness of my own sinfulness. God used the sharing of His Word and the confession of His people as a searchlight to shine deeply into all our hearts. I found myself weeping over things that God was showing me about my heart and my motives. It brought to mind something I had heard J. Edwin Orr say: When we pray for revival, most of us don't have any idea what we are praying for. His point was that we think we are praying for ecstasy—and yes, joy is a by-product of revival—but revival does not begin in ecstasy, but in agony.

I think it was this overwhelming sense of God's holy presence that protected us from an atmosphere of judgmentalism in the meetings. There is ordinarily no lack of judgmentalism on our campus; yet that night (and throughout the week) it was strangely absent. I think all of us present felt the weight of the words of the song, "It's not my brother, not my sister, but it's *me,* O Lord, standing in the need of prayer."

I left at about 4:00 A.M., but the meeting was still going strong. My wife, Sharon, had taken our car and gone home at midnight. Lyle Dorsett, another faculty member, drove me home. We tried to put into words what we were sensing; we both agreed that God was doing a deep work. We prayed for protection from the attacks of Satan on our campus. Little did I know this would become the pattern for the week.

MONDAY, MARCH 20

The 10:30 A.M. chapel service was abuzz with excitement. Even those who weren't at the WCF meeting had heard by now what had taken place. Chaplain Kellough shared with the entire campus community what had happened the night (and early morning) before. His words paint a vivid picture of events, and they offer sound counsel for follow-up:

> Most of you know that last evening's WCF meeting was an incredible, wonderful time of spiritual refreshment. There were tears and there were smiles. There was crying, there was singing. People confessed their sins to God. People confessed their sins to each other. There was healing. There was worship, there was Scripture, there was prayer, there was the public confession of sin, and there was forgiveness. It was biblical, it was Christian, it was orderly, it was sincere; I believe that it honored God. The program last night began at 7:30, but the meeting ended at 6:00 this morning.
>
> In the wake of this remarkable work of God in the hearts of so many people, I would like to share three things to keep in mind this morning. First, after a time of spiritual refreshment, and I believe that is what we had—a time of spiritual refreshment—we should expect the attack of the enemy. We should expect it! Last night there was a lot of talk about spiritual warfare and many prayers focused on this very issue. At times like these, we should expect the enemy to hammer us, especially this morning I think. The enemy would like nothing more than to give doubts to the legitimacy of spiritual experience in our life with

God.

Second, we cannot manufacture spiritual awakening. Last night many people raised the caution of manipulation. Those who were there would certainly testify to the spiritual validity of what happened. And so, be encouraged by the Scripture; be encouraged by your Christian friends; be encouraged by the Holy Spirit, and do not be discouraged by the enemy. Since we cannot manufacture spiritual awakening, periods of spiritual refreshment may be long, or they may be short. We need to acknowledge the work of God that is the work of God—and we cannot bring spiritual awakening by ourselves any more than we can regenerate the heart of an unbeliever. That is the work of God the Holy Spirit.

Third, after a time of spiritual awakening, we need to keep on praying. The experience of some can cause the rest of us to pray for our entire campus and for our world.

Chaplain Kellough then prayed for protection and for a continued work of God on the campus.

I arrived at Pierce Chapel Monday evening at about 8:45 P.M. to pray and reflect on what was happening. Students began pouring into the auditorium at about 9:15 P.M. Immediately I was struck by the fact that many of them were carrying Bibles. Wheaton students have Bibles, but they don't always bring them to meetings. Yet student after student walked in with a Bible. It suddenly hit me—this was one of Jonathan Edwards' "Distinguishing Marks of a Work of the Spirit of God"! Edwards penned this classic work during the First Great Awakening (1741) to help people distinguish a genuine work of God from mere emotionalism. I retraced in my mind Edward's five distinguishing marks of a genuine work of God:

1. It raises the esteem of Jesus;

2. Satan's kingdom suffers as the Spirit of God strikes out against sin;

3. Men and women will have a greater respect for Scripture;

4. Men and women will see more clearly spiritual truth and error;

5. There will be a new sense of love toward God and others.

I sat in quiet gratitude as I reflected on what I had seen on our campus and how it mirrored these marks of revival as delineated by Jonathan Edwards.

Matt Yarrington shared for a few minutes, highlighting that this was not something that WCF had done—this was the work of God. His remarks were met by thunderous applause. Matt encouraged the group to focus on three things in the days ahead: prayer, the Scriptures, and mutual accountability.

Matt went on to make a distinction between remorse and repentance, between merely feeling sorry for our sin and genuinely turning from it. He challenged people only to confess publicly if they were truly repentant— not only sorry for their sin but ready to turn from it. He referred to things people may have in their dorm rooms as "hidden provisions for defeat"—things that would trip them up in the days ahead. A student then read from Mark 9:42-47 and talked about getting rid of the things that cause us to stumble. He and another student brought some secular CDs and placed them on the stage as a symbol of giving them to God.

Matt told the group that they did not want to give the impression that everyone had to give up secular music to get right with God, but that they did need to give up whatever was causing them to stumble. He mentioned that they would start a pile on the stage and asked another student to go and get some garbage bags to collect the "stuff." He also asked those present who had already confessed and who did not have an account-ability partner or group to raise their hands. He then asked others around them to pray for them and to consider playing that vital role in their lives.

Matt expressed his desire that this be a lasting work and then led in prayer to that end. He asked those confessing to be as brief as possible because many others wanted to confess. From that point forward, the meeting continued along the same lines as the previous evening. Student after student confessed sin and received prayer and encouragement from others. At about 1:45 A.M. it was announced that we would have two more confessions and then dismiss for the evening, reconvening again at 9:30 P.M. that evening. Dozens of students were still in line at the microphones.

The pile of "stuff" on the stage was both encouraging and depressing. Books, magazines, videos, alcohol, drugs, CDs, a credit card (symbolizing a bondage to materialism), a rose (symbolizing a destructive relationship)—these and many other items were placed there by students wanting to get right with God. It was wonderful to see how deeply God was at work; it was depressing to see what people had been hiding away in their rooms. It took five garbage bags to gather up all the "stuff." After a prayer of dedication, it was taken far away from campus and destroyed.

The meeting concluded by singing "How Great Thou Art" and "Amazing Grace." These great hymns of the faith were requested by students as the language with which they wanted to express their praise and worship to God.

TUESDAY, MARCH 21

We discovered that Pierce Chapel would not be available that evening because of a scheduling conflict. Where would we meet? College Church, located right across the street, (though not affiliated with the college), graciously allowed WCF to use their auditorium. The move was providential, for more than thirteen hundred people came to the meeting. Had the meeting been held in Pierce Chapel, several hundred would have been turned away. Also, the wide and spacious hallways outside the main auditorium of College Church gave abundant space for small groups to meet for confession, prayer, encouragement, and follow-up.

The meeting began with praise and worship. Song after song testified to the wonder of God's grace and His work in our lives. Matt Yarrington spoke briefly before the time of confession began. He shared Jonathan Edward s "Distinguishing Marks of a Work of the Spirit of God" and talked about how we had seen them evident in our midst. People responded with loud, lengthy, standing applause.

Matt then read Matthew 12:43-45 and expressed a concern about having an emptying without a corresponding filling. He said, "We need to be filling our lives with the things of God as we are emptying it of the things of the world." He again stressed the importance of Bible reading, prayer, and accountability groups.

Again, the microphones were opened for students to confess. Throughout the evening confessions of sin were interspersed with testimonies of victory, songs and the reading of Scripture.

Kevin Engel noted that many people had come from other campuses and churches as word about what was taking place had spread. He asked for these people to stand and then asked for others to gather around them and pray that they might see an outpouring of the Spirit of God on their campus or in their church. The meeting ended around 2:00 A.M. with a time of singing.

WEDNESDAY, MARCH 22

At Wednesday morning's chapel service, Chaplain Kellough gave an update to the entire campus community about what had taken place the two previous nights and invited all who wanted to participate to come to College Church at 9:30 P.M.

Following the chapel, Kellough asked Kevin Engel, Matt Yarrington, Lyle Dorsett, John Fawcett (the Head of Public Services for Buswell Library), and me to meet with him briefly. While we had kept in touch informally throughout each day (and night!), this was the first "planning meeting" since the beginning of the revival. We all sat down, caught our breath, and began to discuss what God was doing on our campus and where we sensed things should go from here.

Two decisions were made, both by consensus. First, it was determined that the evening meetings would continue as long as there were students still lined up to confess sin when we dismissed the group early in the morning. We did not want to rob people of the opportunity to confess their sins publicly if that was what they felt God was leading them to do.

Second, we felt the need to provide further instruction for those who had already confessed sin and gotten right with God and others. Kevin Engel and Matt Yarrington had done a wonderful job weaving advice throughout the three previous sessions. Chaplain Kellough had offered wise counsel during his opening remarks in the Monday and Wednesday morning chapel sessions, but Wednesday night would provide a strategic setting to provide specific guidance to the students.

That evening, the president of Wheaton College, Dr. Duane Litfin, spoke to the crowd. He previously had stayed away from the meeting for fear of making the students self-conscious about their confession. When he learned that some were interpreting his absence at the previous meetings as a lack of support, he came to communicate his support. He shared from Isaiah 6, challenging the people to keep their eyes on the Lord. He concluded by saying, "You have my blessing on what is taking place here—but more importantly, you have God's blessing."

I then shared a list of key principles in dealing with temptation, focusing on concepts such as: recognizing you are in a battle (Eph. 6:12; 1 Pet. 5:8); understanding the process of temptation (Gen. 3:1-6); protecting your mind (Rom. 16:19; 1 Cor. 10:12; Phil. 4:8); avoiding tempting circumstances (Prov. 27:12; Matt. 5:29-30; 26:41); removing hidden provisions for defeat (Eph. 4:27; Rom. 13:14); deciding in advance what you will do in a tempting situation (1 Tim. 6:11; 2 Tim. 2:22; 1 Cor. 6:18); and memorizing God's Word (Eph. 6:17; Ps. 119:9-11).

After listening to several confessions, I left the auditorium and talked with various students in the hallway to get a better idea of what was happening on our campus outside the evening meetings. A resident advisor in a dormitory told me a guy on his floor with a "stone-cold heart" was converted the night before. Another student shared with me about feeling impressed to go talk with a girl on her dorm floor who was not walking with Christ. She ran across campus, praying the entire way that God would prepare this girl's heart. When she knocked on the door, she heard a muffled "come in." This girl was sitting on her bed with her Bible, weeping. She said she had prayed that God would send someone to talk to her—that she had many needs in her life and she needed help. Story after story could be told of God's work in reconciling people to Himself and to others. Later in the evening Lyle Dorsett shared with the group on "Where Do We Go from Here," emphasizing the themes of prayer, Bible study, accountability, and involvement in a local church. About 1:50 A.M. the last student in line to confess sin had done so. A decision was made to meet again the following night at 9:30 P.M. for a testimony and praise service.

THURSDAY, MARCH 23

As we gathered in College Church for the evening session, there was a spirit of expectation. We wanted to express our praise to our gracious God who had touched us in a beautiful way this week. Having seen the ugliness of our sin, the contrast of the beauty of Christ and His work was clearly in focus. We sang—and sang—and sang some more. Particularly memorable were the words to the second verse of "It Is Well with My Soul":

My sin, O the bliss of this glorious thought
My sin, not in part, but the whole Is
nailed to the cross, and I bear it no more
Praise the Lord, praise the Lord, O my
soul!

Matt Yarrington requested that if there were still those who wanted to confess sin, that they invite a few others to go out in the hallway with them where they could freely talk. Matt reminded us that we don't need public confession every time we sin. We need to go to God each time we sin, but not necessarily to each other. Kellough preached a message from Ephesians 3, giving specific guidance about walking with Christ daily.

Several students then testified to a victory in their lives or to how they had seen God at work. It was a powerfully moving time. One graduate student testified about how she had trusted Christ for salvation during the week. She had never seen herself as sinful and had never truly professed faith in Christ for salvation until this week. Another student told of reconciliation with his father. Many other joyful testimonies followed.

A graduate student from Indonesia, Leo Sumule, quoted Isaiah 6:8 and challenged the group to say, "Here am I—send me." Jeanne Blumhagen, a trustee of the college and a former missionary, shared after Leo. She began her comments by saying, "God is here." She challenged students to open their eyes to the harvest fields of the world and then led in prayer.

At the suggestion of a student, Matt Yarrington

offered an invitation to make a commitment to full-time ministry. Between two and three hundred gathered at the front and up the center aisle of the church. Matt Yarrington and Lyle Dorsett led in a prayer of dedication for these students who had committed themselves to take the gospel to the ends of the earth.

We concluded with a time of praise and worship that I thought was literally going to raise the roof! It wasn't simply the volume, though it was loud. It was the difference between merely singing and truly praising—and we were praising our wonderful God who had graciously visited us during the week.

A scene I will never forget took place during the song, "Our God Reigns." Pat Bell, a graduate student headed for the mission field, went up on the stage and began waving the Christian flag as a testimony to the sovereign rule of God over this world. It was a beautiful expression of worship.

Nate Fawcett closed the meeting at about 12:45 A.M. by praying, "What more can we say, except, 'Thank You, Jesus!'"

Sharon and I stayed until 2:00 A.M., not simply because of our newly formed habit, but because we just did not want to leave!

THE DAYS FOLLOWING

Different entities on our campus sought to encourage the students in the days following the revival. Early morning meetings were set up in the residence halls for students who wanted to pray, study the Scriptures, and be in an accountability relationship. About forty faculty members met to discuss what they could do to encourage students. The staff of the Student Development Department and the Counseling Center were doing what they could to encourage and help students.

Requests began to pour in for Wheaton students to go to other places to share. At last count they have visited more than forty schools and churches. Many of these places are experiencing a similar outpouring of God's Spirit. And so the story continues.

March 19-24 was an incredible week in all our lives. On Thursday evening we sang "Let Your Glory Fall," just as we had on Sunday. The words took on an even deeper meaning as we sang together:

Let Your glory fall in this room
Let it flow forth from here to the nations
Let Your fragrance rest in this place
As we gather to seek Your face.

God in His wonderful grace chose to answer that prayer "exceedingly abundantly" beyond all we could have ever hoped for or dreamed.

No human being orchestrated these events; all of us were amazed at what our gracious and sovereign God had done in our midst. "This was the LORD'S doing; it is marvelous in our eyes"(Ps. 118:23).

CHAPTER 12
A WHEATON STUDENT'S JOURNAL

MATT YARRINGTON

The following selections from my journals tell of the recent revival. Some of the entries, including those surrounding the week of March 19, were not written on the day they appear. The events of that week did not allow much time for journaling.

Many others could write similar accounts, and hundreds of other students from Wheaton have spoken in churches, universities, and other places across the country.

Monday, February 13, 1995. I am enjoying the class on History and Theology of Revival. Soon I will have to choose my personal reading project for the class—five hundred pages plus a paper. I have pretty much decided on doing Charles G. Finney's *Lectures on Revivals of Religion.* I read somewhere that it is the "most influential work" ever written on the topic, and it's just over five hundred pages.

Today I interviewed Dr. and Mrs. Ray Ortlund, Sr., by telephone. I was amazed to hear their story of the 1970 revival at Wheaton. Even though they were the special speakers invited for the Spiritual Emphasis week, they did not even speak when the night of revival came. Their experiences during those days completely changed the direction of their lives together and especially their ministry. *Praise You, Lord!*

Thursday, March 2. An amazing thing happened today. Several students and Dr. Beougher received faxes and phone calls last night from friends at Southwestern Baptist Theological Seminary. A revival broke out there yesterday. Apparently, two students from Howard Payne University went to Southwestern and spoke in classes about the revival at their school. Dr. John Avant preached in chapel. Students were so moved that public confessions of sin resulted. The school president even canceled classes as students began to get right with God.

Dr. Beougher was excited about this because Southwestern is his alma mater. A friend of his who teaches there phoned him to say that this is "the real thing." I must admit, I had a hard time getting as excited as many in the class because I am a bit skeptical about "real" revival. Especially if it might just be humanly orchestrated.

Things became personal quite fast, however. Dr. Beougher turned to me in all this excitement and said, "You know, Matt, World Christian Fellowship (I serve as student chair) is one of the most spiritually sensitive groups on campus. If you would like to fly a couple of students up here from Howard Payne to speak on what God is doing on their campus, I would be willing to pay for it out of my personal savings. Of course, I'm not *asking* you to do it, but if you'd like to, I can arrange it."

My first thought was, *doesn't Dr. Beougher know that we plan our speakers a semester in advance? Our worship leaders have their final song agendas turned in two weeks before each event, and today is the deadline for our next service.* But I knew that this could be the divine hand of Providence at work.

Convinced that something (or Someone) bigger than

I or WCF was at work, I determined to ask the WCF Cabinet at our afternoon meeting if we could postpone our scheduled events for the next Sunday meeting (March 19, the Sunday after spring break), and invite some students from Texas to speak.

At the cabinet meeting, Doug O'Donnell, a worship leader, discussed what had happened in class. This was uncharted territory. Just as our discussion reached an impasse Dr. Beougher came through the door unannounced. Talk about timing! I had given him a voice mail forty-five minutes earlier asking him to stop by if he had the chance, to help explain things a little. Providentially, he was there.

He helped answer our questions. It was rather exciting, even a little scary. After our positive vote to invite the students, we knew that one other person had to pass it—my administrative advisor, Kevin Engel. If he passes it, we'll have two students from Texas in two weeks.

Kevin was understandably shaken to hear of our maverick decision, yet I assured him that we all understood the buck stopped with him. We would wait for his approval. I asked him to call Dr. Beougher since he could explain things much better. That was at 5:00 P.M.

Thank You, Lord Jesus. Lord, I pray Your will be done now. Alleluia, Amen.

Saturday, March 4. Finney says a "convergence of Providence" often precedes a powerful revival. Christians who have their eyes open to these providential factors often know when a revival is just around the corner. I sense that this is happening right now. Too much is happening all at once for this just to be coincidence.

Meanwhile, I have been busy gathering information and coordinating flights for two Howard Payne students named Jay and Brandi. Yesterday (Tuesday) I spoke with Dr. Doug Munton, a pastor in Texas who is a Wheaton graduate. Jay spoke at his church recently, and Dr. Munton couldn't say enough to recommend him to us.

Father, please let these students come to Wheaton. Please move in power. Touch Your people in a way that we would not believe, even if it were told us in advance. Do something in our midst, Lord, that has never been seen before. Father, I do not ask for a repeat of the revivals of 1970 or 1950. I'm asking for something new, unprecedented, and incalculable. Glorify Your name as never before at our school. And please, Lord, raise up workers for Your name. Alleluia! Come, Lord Jesus.

WHEATON COLLEGE

Wednesday, March 15. Monday, Kevin and I decided how to publicize this week's Sunday night: "When God Moves: Two students from a university in Texas tell how God recently brought revival to their campus." I like that title. It's not past tense; it leaves room for God to move again!

Tomorrow I fast and pray for our school as usual. Saturday night, Nate Fawcett and I will pick up Jay and Brandi from the airport. PTL! Jay will stay in my room, which I am greatly looking forward to. Brandi is staying with Claudia Lopez.

I sent out today a special letter to the fifty-plus leaders working with WCF encouraging them to (1) be in special prayer and fasting for God to move in power this weekend, (2) search their own hearts and repent of all known sins in preparation for God's visitation, and (3) invite someone who usually doesn't come to this Sunday's meeting. I can sense rising anticipation among many students for this weekend, as I have heard people talking about this event.

Sunday, March 19, 6:00 P.M. Last night we picked up Brandi and Jay. We had a very good time of getting to know them. They are both very normal people—as in, not incredibly different from us—very friendly.

I'm enjoying just getting to know Jay. He has a certain boldness that I haven't experienced in anyone else (except Brandi). We can be talking about any number of topics, but when it comes time to talk about the movement of the Holy Spirit, especially as it pertains to this revival phenomenon, I find myself with nothing to say, only listening.

As the moderator for the evening, I asked how to proceed when they finished speaking. They were very specific in stating that my role should be to do as little as possible (stay out of the way) and let the Spirit have His own way in people's lives. They said it was important to remain open, in case God moved in people's hearts. The key was openness.

PIERCE CHAPEL

Sunday Night, March 19. God moved! Nate Fawcett began with a very important sketch of our evening in order to calm fears that we were trying to re-create anything such as a revival. We proceeded with the worship time, singing praise songs and then some songs of personal preparation and reflection.

Nate introduced the speakers. First Brandi spoke. The Holy Spirit was moving in power, convicting hearts of sin, laziness, apathy, and more. When she finished, I sensed that every throat was choked with conviction of sin and with the testimony of God's power to change lives. She was genuine and spoke with the presence of the Holy Spirit. Next, Jay spoke with equal conviction about changed lives in his church, at Howard Payne, and at other colleges. Based on James 5:16, he outlined a three-step process: "Confess your trespasses to one another, and pray for one another"—He told how Christians of all ages and types were beginning to take off masks, repent of sins, clean up their lives, and become accountable to each other in prayer.

1. "That you may be healed"—He gave examples of how these same students had been freed from long-term addictions and every imaginable sin, because they were following the biblical procedure of confession and repentance.

2. "The effective fervent prayer of a righteous person avails much"—Jay pointed out that once we are right with God and each other, our prayers take on a new dimension of power. He gave amazing testimony to God answering the prayers of newly revived Christians in miraculous ways and of many people coming to Christ due to cleaned-up Christians who began to pray with new power.

Jay ended with a direct challenge to let God have His own way with our lives. He encouraged us to follow the pattern presented by the Scripture. Then he sat down. The house was very still as I got up to speak. I could feel conviction in the air, including my own. After praying, I invited any who wanted to respond to what we heard to do so at the two microphones in front. Students were told they could ask questions, pray, confess sin, or respond in any way they felt led, if at all.

Students began coming forward immediately to confess sin. After one or two confessions, I asked volunteers to pray with the confessors, in keeping with the James 5:16 model. For the rest of the night, indeed, until 6:00 A.M., students stood in line to confess sin, while those who had confessed were surrounded by loving and praying students. My role consisted of simply offering necessary reminders on occasion, such as, "Only confess your own sin, not those of others." Kevin Engel, my advisor, was there to trade places with me throughout the night.

So many men confessed sexual sins and addictions of various types that Jay invited all men struggling with lust and sexual sins to come forward and pray together. About fifty men rushed to the front. Pricked by the scene of the men kneeling in repentance, women began to stand and confess that it was not only the men who sinned in these areas. Some confessed of wearing inappropriate clothing in order to get attention. Other sins were confessed as well. There was more weeping, brokenness, and prayer.

Around 10:00 P.M., at Kevin's suggestion, I made it clear that people were free to leave, though we would continue. Strangely, the crowd increased because some students went to call friends and roommates. I told students that I didn't believe God had come in power to touch half of the campus, but that He wanted the whole school to receive the benefit.

At 6:00 A.M., Kevin and I, with other advisors like Chaplain Kellough, decided to dismiss students. Those who wanted to do so were told they could return at 9:30 in the evening, especially those still waiting to confess. We didn't want to deny anyone the opportunity for confession and getting their lives right with God and with each other. *Praise to You, Lord Christ! Amen.*

Monday Night, March 20. Tonight's meeting went from 9:30 P.M. until 2:00 A.M. Contrary to my expectation, more people came than on Sunday night—a few hundred more. The evening began with praise and worship with Nate and his team as leaders.

Tonight two students (Eric Gorman and Dave Terry) came forward to ask me a question privately. Although students were getting their lives clean, they explained there were still many things in their rooms waiting to "get" them. Couldn't we have a way to get rid of items that might cause people to continue stumbling? I asked them to get some garbage bags and come back. Eric made the announcement, and then dumped a backpack full of stuff onto the stage.

By the end of the evening, five garbage bags were filled with hundreds of CDs, clothing, magazines (representing materialism for some), alcohol, pornography, lists of sins on paper, and more. The only guidelines I made were "things you know will cause you to stumble, or things the Spirit brings to your mind that you need to get rid of." After we closed the evening, I asked some students to dispose of the bags "far from the college," which they did. *Praise to You, Lord Jesus!*

Tuesday Night, March 21. Today we were providentially displaced from Pierce Chapel.

After a few more brief comments and reminders, I

opened the evening for students to continue with confessions. We made a special point to allow those who ended last night in line to return to the line first.

Wednesday Night, March 22. This morning after chapel, Dr. Beougher, Dr. Dorsett, Dr. Kellough, Kevin, John Fawcett, and I met for prayer, to discern where to go from here. We are at an important juncture. As our Lord taught, if we don't fill our cleaned-out houses, the last state will become worse than the first (Matt. 12:43-45).

I mentioned that all teaching should be at the beginning of the evening, or students would be off praying and miss out. Dr. Litfin, the president of the college, would begin (after worship time). Then Dr. Beougher would give a short teaching on how to battle temptation. He had prepared a handout entitled "Ten Ways to Avoid Temptation."

It was very encouraging to see the president there. I praise the Lord for such a leader as Dr. Litfin, who is truly behind the work of God's Spirit. I was thankful for his encouraging words to the body tonight, as he said he was behind what was happening and longed to be more involved, though he didn't want to get in the way.

I was very hesitant to be up front tonight. I asked Kevin if I could be excused from any up-front duties from here on out. He graciously took the position of moderator for nearly the whole evening. However, he said he needed to be relieved near the end. At 2:05 A.M. the last young man waiting in line had his chance to confess his sin. No doubt, this was a happy moment for Kevin and me. Twenty-one hours of confession! We ended with a few choruses of praise and thanksgiving then left, proclaiming the following evening as a night for celebration for what the Lord had begun to accomplish in our midst.

Thursday, March 23. After our opening praise and worship, Chaplain Kellough spoke from Ephesians 3 on continuing to grow in the grace of God. He underscored the importance of turning this week's experiences into lifelong changes.

Tonight the microphones were opened for this, our last plenary session. But instead of repentance, testimonies focused on praise for how God had worked in lives this week. Students told of relationships healed with family and friends, of addictions conquered, and more. Throughout the evening, different students broke away from the theme to exhort the body of the needs for evangelism that exist in the world.

When I arrived tonight and prayed with the circle of advisors who helped throughout the week (Dr. Dorsett, Dr. Beougher, John Fawcett, and others), each one said that they were impressed with the need to evangelize that very day. Even our prayers before the service began were fervent that God would raise up workers.

As we neared the end of the confession time, a college trustee who was a veteran missionary was invited to address the group. She gave a very meaningful thought about the needs of the world for Christ. She issued a challenge to consider our part in fulfilling the Great Commission. As the last students were testifying (we had set a time limit so we could end at a decent hour), Kevin and I received a note from an anonymous student that read: "As a suggestion: You could have those who want to devote their lives to full-time Christian service come to the front to kneel and be prayed over." Kevin looked at me and asked, "What do you think?" I said, "It's now or never." I made the announcement quietly, almost in monotone. Immediately, perhaps two hundred and fifty students came forward and flooded the aisles, at least as far back as the middle of the sanctuary. Dr. Dorsett, overcome with emotion, gave a prayer of thanksgiving for these workers, and dedication of our lives to full-time service in the King's militia. I praise the Lord for students, faculty, the collective wisdom of the body, and the inner promptings of His Holy Spirit.

Can I remember or imagine a time of worship more celestial than this evening? No, I cannot. Our closing songs focused on going out into the world.

Before Dr. Beougher left for the night, he approached me to say two things: "Matt, pack your bags; and get ready for the calls." He was expecting our office to receive a ton of calls, asking Wheaton students about what is happening. I reflected for a bit on how this is the lightest academic load I have ever taken, and yet I chose this before the revival, for completely different reasons. Perhaps this is another sign of God's providence.

CHANNEL 38

Wednesday Morning, March 29. Three fellow students and I talked with David Mains on his national TV broadcast about the events at Wheaton. The four of us prayed together before the show, asking God to use it to glorify His Name and encourage His people across the country toward confession and repentance. Praise You, Lord Jesus.

NORTH PARK COLLEGE, CHICAGO

Wednesday Night, March 29. A professor of Youth Ministry at North Park College had been approached by students in recent weeks for a special meeting for the purpose of waiting on the Lord and listening to two Wheaton students tell about the revival at Wheaton. This was my first opportunity to speak about what the Lord has done here on campus. Saranell Kracht went with me. We arrived for the meeting scheduled to begin at 9:00 P.M. Saranell and I spent some time in prayer after we met the leader and some of the students. The meeting was fashioned after a "concert of prayer." After perhaps an hour of singing and various times of small group praying, we were asked to share.

I talked about what revival is and is not. Then I told them about what happened during the revival week at Wheaton, including a few highlights. I ended by sharing the two Scriptures most important to me in these days—James 5:16, and 1 Peter 4:17. After that, Saranell spoke on how sin isolates but how confession and repentance bring together. She then shared still more highlights.

Afterward, the leader left the microphone open for anyone who had anything to share. There were exhortations, stories, Scripture readings, and other thoughts. One student made a confession and asked for prayer; the students prayed for her (there were about thirty students gathered). Saranell and I left just before they were finished at midnight.

We did not see revival in the manner that we saw it at Wheaton. However, if I did suppose that our words had any power to cause this revival to manifest itself, I was proven wrong.

I was somewhat disheartened. The Lord knows, and perhaps it was the best thing that could have happened on my first time speaking about the revival to keep me humble. Saranell reminded me tonight that perhaps the reason the Lord had us come here was just to encourage someone to pray more. If that is true, then our work is vindicated. I think she is right. *Praise the Lord.*

Thursday, March 30. I received a call to do a telephone interview with Bill and Vonette Bright this week. I had the chance to share with them and their radio audience. They were very encouraged because they have been praying and fasting for spiritual awakening in North America. Dr. Bright asked me if I would mind if he sent us a thousand free copies of his new book, *The Coming Revival.* I assured him students would use them. He asked me to be sure to only give them to those who would read them. *Praise to You, Lord Jesus!*

One comment that Dr. Bright said will stick with me for a long time. "Matt, as someone who has evaluated every day of my life for the last forty years in light of the Great Commission, ..."I don't remember how he finished that sentence, but I won't forget the example of that kind of life statement.

NORTHWESTERN COLLEGE, MINNEAPOLIS

Monday, April 3. Today I flew to Minneapolis with Elizabeth Simpson. We spoke in the chapel service at 10:00 A.M. After we finished, the student leader, Dave Spooner, told the group in a very matter-of-fact way, "You can leave now. Or you can stay. We don't want to try to concoct anything here. But on the other hand, if God is touching you, we don't want to quench His Spirit either. So I'm just going to leave the microphone open." With that he sat down!

I think two people left. What resulted was a massive movement of the Holy Spirit that "leveled their campus," as Elizabeth said. Students of all classes and associations confessed sins of every type. Prayer was happening everywhere. The movement was deep, very deep. We had the chance to eat a late lunch with the Student Government president and gave him some ideas about how to follow-up the confessions. We had to leave the campus at 5:00 P.M., but I learned later that services continued for another day. Student government, professors, and administrators were all involved in building follow-up opportunities for students to maintain their commitments and receive special help or accountability. Eventually, students from Northwestern were taking their own message of revival to the surrounding Christian churches and universities, with revival resulting. We left in awe, unable to put into words our emotions or what we had experienced.

GORDON COLLEGE AND EASTERN NAZARENE COLLEGE, MASSACHUSETTS

Wednesday, April 5. At Gordon, Dr. Beougher and I were welcomed by Gary Stratton, dean of the chapel, and student leaders. We met with Brandi Maguire and Chris Robeson, the student who "started" this confessional revival in his Texas church. He is humble, genuine.

Dr. Beougher spoke to the faculty, while seven of us were praying for them. He told me it was a good and fruitful meeting. We went to the new chapel at 10:00 P.M. for the special meeting where we were to speak. Chris, Brandi, and I shared. Student testimonies began. There was deep conviction, repentance, confession, prayer, and healing. I retired at 12:30 with thirty people still waiting in line.

One of the greatest blessings for me on this trip is getting to know Gary Stratton. He is intensely humble. He actually took my hands tonight at dinner and asked my forgiveness for his jealousy toward me (!) for getting to be a student leader during God's powerful work at Wheaton (he is an alum). When Gary prayed at dinner, he prayed with greater faith than I have ever seen regarding the *finishing* of Christ's Great Commission! I've thought it, but I can't remember ever having such powerful belief as to pray publicly and boldly for it.

Thursday, April 6. This morning I left for Eastern Nazarene College in Boston with Dean Gary Stratton, Chris, and Brandi. ENC was incredible. We shared at their chapel service. I felt great and unusual freedom, calmness, and power as I spoke the Word of God with boldness.

What followed was a picture of the Wheaton revival. Confessions were deep and profound.

Thursday Night, April 6. Gary Stratton is quite an amazing man of God. He told me today that he is on the thirty-seventh day of a forty-day fast. God will honor him for his service of faith. He is so "on our level" in how he relates to us, very humble and others-centered. I have much to learn from him.

Tonight was the second night of special meetings in the chapel at Gordon. I'm so surprised, but God is not going to fit into our mold. He is doing something different here than at Wheaton. This revival is quiet. The whole campus has yet to be affected. It is not awakening yet, although those seeking Jesus are being cleansed and purged mightily.

MOODY BIBLE INSTITUTE, CHICAGO

Thursday, April 13. Today I spoke in Moody's chapel together with fellow Wheaton student, Kate Amerlan. David Martin, the leader of Student Missions

Fellowship, had invited us to come and share in the SMF chapel. Confessions of sin resulted, though not all the students stayed. Confessions continued into the afternoon and will resume after the Easter break.

OTHER CAMPUSES

Thursday, April 20. We arrived at Messiah College, Grantham, Pennsylvania. Before the services, we prayed together and then proceeded to Grantham Chapel for the 8:30 service.

I spoke first, and then Mark. God came in power to Powerhouse. There was heartfelt repentance and James 5:16 healing going on. A deep work! Cheri said tonight's Powerhouse attendance was the largest she had ever seen. I estimate five hundred students. The place was packed. Praise You, Lord.

The living, moving body of Christ became reality tonight. Mark and I assisted Christa Ann during the first hour or so. She is a very capable leader. We retired at midnight to Greenbriar.

Friday, April 21, Columbia University, New York. I went to sleep this morning at 3:45 A.M., with the sound of praise choruses wafting over the spring hills toward Greenbriar and through my open window. The redeemed were ending their meeting with God—for now!

The evening meeting was very different from anything I have experienced so far. Thirty students! A deep but quiet work of God among them! The evening of confessions was gentle, very real, and thoroughly powerful.

I drove to Yale late in the night, where I met Paul Maykish, my host. I'm staying here in the Divinity school. Maranatha.

Saturday, April 22, Yale University. At the service tonight, perhaps one hundred and fifty students plus others filled Timothy Dwight Memorial Chapel. Mel told everyone the purpose for the evening; it was so well done that it set everyone at ease. After some singing of reflective worship songs, Paul introduced me.

After sharing the Wheaton story and others, I gave some historical reflection on Yale's previous awakenings, on Timothy Dwight's presidency here, and the revival of 1802 (the pinnacle of the Second Great Awakening). I ended with the challenge I give everywhere, using James 5:16 and 1 Peter 4:17.

After that, Brandon Bayne from Columbia shared some reflections from the night before, telling how God had moved among the group at Columbia. He spoke on sin's isolation and the true meaning of the unity of the body of Christ. Afterward, Mel got up to say, "That's all our input tonight. You're free to go, or you're welcome to stay here as we enter a time of prayer and waiting on the Lord." As far as I know, no one left.

Several prayed spontaneously. Someone shared a dream that when students in Dwight Chapel were invited to ask for prayer for their hardness of heart, or "cold hearts toward God," that revival would come. Mel invited those present who wanted prayer for this to raise their hands. All over the room, circles of prayer resulted around those who had raised their hands. This prayer lasted for perhaps forty-five minutes. Many circles broke into spontaneous confession of sin within the small groups.

Later, Brandon and I became convicted that there were sins that needed to be confessed corporately. After some songs of worship and refocus, Brandon, and then I, rose to give exhortation.

The result was perhaps twenty-five heartfelt, broken, and deep public confessions of sins of pride, prejudice, and especially reconciliation between Christian groups at odds with one another. The whole gamut of sins that have been confessed around the country were confessed tonight. Weeping and prayer and healing were the results as students ministered to one another. I praised God, but I wept inwardly for those students, perhaps a third, who had already left and not witnessed this phase of God's work this evening.

My heart was yearning beyond degree that the entire body of Christ at Yale might truly experience the unity and full love for one another that Jesus prayed for in John 17, which unity these confessions created so joyfully and brilliantly. For as our Lord Jesus said, by this all will know that He is true and from the Father. I envisioned the power of the body to shine forth to the rest of the university, and a result of many conversions bringing glory to Christ, massive glory.

I am told that this evening's event is unprecedented in the memories of all those present. Christian groups came together that before had refused completely to associate. Dwight Chapel had not had a "Call to Prayer" that drew out all the Christian groups on campus in recent years. This was a big step toward unity. Praise the Lord!

The meeting spontaneously lasted until 2:45 A.M. as students began to lead out in worship to God that was an experience indeed! After that, no one dismissed the group. It was as if everyone felt the Holy Spirit had taken complete control and finally dismissed us for the evening. Students left in joy.

Sunday, April 23. Paul Maykish is my host. He spoke in

church today, his last time speaking here as a student. He was indescribable in the pulpit. A message fit for an audience of ten thousand, given lovingly to ten. He fasted for more than two days for that message. This man has spiritual power combined with meekness, the likes of which I've never seen.

On the plane home I read this verse given to me for today by someone at Wheaton: "Your love, O Lord, reaches to the heavens, your faithfulness to the skies. Your righteousness is like the mighty mountains, your justice like the great deep. O Lord, you preserve both man and beast. How priceless is your unfailing love! Both high and low among men find refuge in the shadow of your wings" (Ps. 36:5-7).

Father, could words ever express Your loving kindness toward me? I do love You. You have been good, have loved me,and better than all, have glorified Yourself using this broken vessel. Thank You, Lord Jesus. Abba. Come.

PART THREE
CONTINUATION

This final section brings the movement of 1995 up-to-date. Our late and beloved professor Roy Fish writes about keeping the flames of revival burning when revival comes. We share what we have learned from then until now, for some things you cannot learn simply by reading history; you have to see them with your own eyes. You will then read some examples of where some of those college students from then are today. Finally, John offers a challenge for revival in our time.

CHAPTER 13
HOW TO KEEP THE FIRE BURNING

ROY FISH
(1930-2012)

God's people pray, travail, perhaps fast, until heaven sends a gracious revival. But once it comes, in time there is a slacking off in intense prayer. Consequently, the blessing is short-lived, and that which could have blessed the church for an extended season lasts for a comparatively short time.

There can be no question that a revival is ultimately the work of God. Revival is new life, and God alone is the giver of this life. But as a rule, God does not work independently of people. This is true both in securing and sustaining revival.

How can revival be sustained? This is one of the most crucial questions about this or any true revival. The movement of revival beginning at Brownwood and spreading across the nation was undoubtedly a work of God's Spirit. What should characterize the response of a church in its efforts to see that revival is ongoing? General revival can actually be sustained for many years. Luther suggested that revival could last thirty years; Wesley said forty years. But even when revival of a general and widespread nature ceases, local churches can continue to live in the experience of awakening. When the tide goes out, it always leaves some pools of water.

Whether locally or generally, the conditions for sustaining revival are basically the same. The conditions for beginning a revival are also the conditions for seeing it perpetuated. People have been challenged with 2 Chronicles 7:14 as the way to experience revival: "If My people who are called by My name will humble themselves, and pray and seek My face, and turn from their wicked ways, then I will hear from heaven, and will forgive their sin and heal their land." If revival is to be sustained, God's people must *remain* humble before Him; they must continue to be steadfast in prayer; they are to be ever seeking the Lord; and they must live lives characterized by repentance of constantly turning from any wicked way. To a degree, the requirements for securing revival become the requirements for sustaining revival.

Revival is a very delicate commodity. It is to be handled with extremely sensitive hands. Some say, "If your revival is really the work of God, it cannot be stopped." This shows a lack of knowledge of both the Bible and history. Not every case in which the story of the current revival was told resulted in a continuous movement of revival. In some cases, powerful services produced no lasting fruit, though in many cases there is fruit that remains.

Exciting new life in the Christian community and numbers of people turning to the Lord irritate the devil. He doesn't take naps during spiritual awakening, and he will do everything he can to stop it. He will oppose it either as a roaring lion or as an angel of light. Churches must be on the guard against his devices and never be surprised at any way he might attempt to interfere with the work of God. Pastors and church leaders must be persons of discernment and firmness—discernment to ascertain what is and what is not of God, and firmness to resist any aspect of revival that is spurious or counterfeit.

GUARDING AGAINST EXTREMES

Revival will be sustained only if extremes are carefully guarded against. Richard Owen Roberts says, "Dealing with extremists and preventing their excesses from disrupting the true work of God in revival are two of the most sensitive and difficult tasks you will ever face; yet they are absolutely mandatory. We must not fail here."[1]

One factor that brought the First Great Awakening in New England to a halt was the contorted demeanor of James Davenport. This preacher claimed that God gave him the gift to determine which preachers were saved and which were lost. He once gathered his rather sizeable congregation and "harangued them for twenty-four hours straight—and then collapsed." Many times he would leave the women in a congregation "fainting and in hysterics," then go singing through the streets. Once he summoned his followers to the wharf at New London, Connecticut, and ordered them to purify themselves from "idolatrous love of worldly things" by burning wigs, fine clothes, jewelry, and dangerous books. The mob then danced around the fire praising God and shouting hallelujah. Davenport later published his retraction, but the damage had been done. Anti-revival forces used Davenport's antics to extinguish the flames of revival. Pastors who want to sustain revival must guard against extremists like James Davenport.

Churches must guard against the antics that characterize the fringes of revival movements. More than one real local church revival has been stifled when well meaning but misled people have invaded services to demonstrate the latest fads of charismania.

REVIVAL AND CONFESSION OF SIN

In the recent moving of God's spirit in revival, public confession has played a very strategic role. This has characterized revivals in the twentieth century in particular. It is a vital part not only of revival beginnings, but of sustaining revival as well. This is in keeping with the admonition of James, "Confess your trespasses to one another, and pray for one another, that you may be healed" (James 5:16). Though some are uneasy about public confession, both the Bible and history justify its merits.

It is obvious that open confession was practiced during the great revival under John the Baptist and in the powerful awakening that shook the city of Ephesus under the apostle Paul (see Acts 20). Confession had its limits, but the need for limiting open confession cannot become an excuse for prohibiting it.

Public confession brings healing to people who have been carrying around spiritual garbage. A part of it may be simply psychological relief, but it also results in tremendous spiritual healing. It also encourages others to confess and forsake sins after a person has publicly confessed failure. In the current movement, those who publicly confess sin have been surrounded by others who pray for them and with them. Someone makes sure that those who have been under deep conviction of sin come to full assurance of forgiveness.

It should be noted that there are obviously dangers in a service where people are permitted or encouraged openly to confess their sins. Public confession, when it gets out of hand, can stop revival. Some unwisely go into lurid detail or become very specific in sins related particularly to sex. It is possible to be discreet in confession of sin in this area, but it must remain very general. Names of others are never to be called in public confession, and almost all sexual offenses should be confessed in secret or in private. "It is shameful even to speak of those things which are done by them in secret" (Eph. 5:12).

In many meetings where public confession is a part, the person in charge, usually the pastor should lay down specific guidelines for public confession. It is wise to set a time limit of three to five minutes for those who will give public testimony. The general rule for confession of sin is: "Let the circle of the sin committed be the circle of the confession made." Secret sins should be confessed in secret. Private sins, those involving other people, should be privately confessed. Open sins, known by a group of people, should be openly confessed. There will, of course, be times when the Holy Spirit may lead a person to set aside this general principle. But a lack of propriety in public confession can bring a serious lack of credibility in what is going on.

ATTITUDE TOWARD OPPOSERS

In almost every revival, some people are suspicious of what is happening. This suspicion sometimes evolves into outright opposition. Often older members of long standing in the church foster this opposition. Abrupt change is painful for some people, and revival in the church always involves change. Sometimes it is a change in methods of worship. Other times there is an obvious new freedom and joy in the hearts of God's people. But change is very unsettling for some and can provoke resistance. When the church is waking up to new life, some obviously waken earlier than others.

Attitudes toward those who are indifferent, suspicious, or resistant to revival are very important. The human tendency is to be very impatient, sometimes vocal in criticizing those who are not in step with what God is doing. But criticizing those who are not yet friends of revival only grieves the Spirit and quenches the fires of revival. A patient, kind, and prayerful spirit toward those who are in opposition will actually perpetuate revival.

Finney said about revival, "While its promoters keep humble, and in a prayerful spirit while they do not retaliate, but possess their souls in patience, while they do not suffer themselves to be diverted, to recriminate, and grieve away the spirit of prayer, the work will go forward."[2]

TEACHING THE WORD AND REVIVAL

The Bible must be central in revival. It must be consistently taught, preached, and privately read if revival is to be sustained. Revival broke out in Brownwood when John Avant began a sermon series on the Ten Commandments.

Richard Owen Roberts, one of the most competent authorities on revival, distinguishes *Word-centered* revivals and *experience-centered* revivals. The Bible will play a role in any revival as will genuine emotion. The question is which will be most prominent. The Word-centered revival is much more prone to last because Bible teaching and preaching take precedence. Experience-centered revivals are usually brief. The Word-centered revival of 1800 lasted forty years. The more experience-centered Welsh revival did a great deal of good, but it was over in two years.

REVIVAL AND PRIDE

Pride will quench the flame of revival. Edwin Orr said in my presence one day, "I have never known of so much prayer for awakening as we are seeing at present. My only fear is that we begin to be proud that we are praying so much."

SUSTAINING REVIVAL THROUGH SHARING

Revival is always enhanced by the willingness of people to share it. Revival comes through prayer, but testimony spreads the flame. This of course has been prominent in the recent awakening. We must, however, be careful in relating what God has been doing. There is a real tendency to exaggerate and "stretch the truth" a bit. Some people can make two converts sound like a reproduction of Nineveh. God's work doesn't need this kind of advertising.

Caution should also be used in exalting new converts. Their testimony is refreshing, but they need time to mature in prayer and Bible study. Putting them in the forefront of a revival may encourage them to neglect their regular development and even swell their heads with pride.

REVIVAL AND WINNING THE LOST

If revival is genuine, lost people will turn to Christ in unusual numbers. Everything in history that is called revival is characterized by large numbers of people turning to Christ. Revival usually creates an unusual

"God consciousness" in a church or a community. It prepares the harvest for reaping. As no other time, God's people should be encouraged to seek to win lost people.

This is what William B. Sprague meant when he said, "Much needs to be done in producing and sustaining a revival by means of *conversation.*" The fervency on a college campus often continues due to ongoing discussions with their peers concerning what God is doing. Pastor Avant continually told his congregation about other revival flare-ups. This has furthered the work in Brownwood.

All believers must willingly engage others in conversation about their spiritual needs. During times of revival, this duty should have a ministry prominent place among Christians; and should not be left to the control of any accidental response. If revival does not make willing converts or empower and enable God's people more faithfully and effectively to share His message with others, then it probably doesn't deserve to be called revival at all.

A pastor is the real key to sustaining revival in a local church. He should encourage special times of prayer and days of fasting and encourage his people through holy living. He should exude optimism that revival will continue and redouble his own efforts in winning people to Christ. John Avant and others set a good example in this revival.

Notes:
1. Richard Owen Roberts, *Revival* (Wheaton: Tyndale House, 1982), pp. 109-10, 117.
2. Charles G. Finney, *Lectures on Revivals of Religion* (Chicago: Fleming H. Revell, 1868), p. 277.

3. William B. Sprague, *Lectures on Revivals of Religion* (New York: Daniel Appleton & Company, 1832), p. 109.

CHAPTER 14
20 YEARS LATER

Some 20 years have passed since God moved in Brownwood and in churches and colleges around the nation. Where are those students now? The following accounts offer only a brief summary taken from interviews with some of those involved in the revival of 1995, telling where they are two decades later.

FROM JAY AND SUSAN, HOWARD PAYNE STUDENTS

[Note: as mentioned earlier, the names of Jay as well as his wife Susan are changed for security reasons]

Now 20 years later, what means the most to you about the revival?

February 14, 1995, is the night the Lord fell on the Howard Payne campus. I remember that afternoon as I was praying and fasting thinking, "I'm a senior. I'm about to graduate. I can wait another couple of months and then get absolutely right with God." But through His conviction I knew that I needed to take the mask of "I have it all together" off. I needed to get right with Him TODAY. He showed me that I needed to confess my sins publicly as mentioned in James 5. I'm so thankful the Lord helped me not to wait because it powerfully impacted my life and the direction of my life. One of the things Henry Blackaby preached that week was that the greatest judgment of God might not be when God shows us all the wrong things we did in our life. The greatest judgment might be when He shows us what 'could have been.' What could have been if we had only obeyed? I look back on the past 20 years of my life, and I'm amazed at how much one step of obedience impacted my life. It impacted who I married, the influential mentors in my life, the calling on my life, and how I try to live my life even today.

How does the revival affect your life now?

I remember Henry Blackaby saying that those who are touched by real revival are never the same. Their lives are different. As our family has spent the last 11 years overseas, with nine of those in the Middle East, my prayer is that the people around us would see God's glory revealed. Whether I'm interacting with cross cultural workers, believing business people, folks in our church, or my children, my prayer for them is to be real. I want them to have accountability partners in their life who will ask them the tough questions, so they don't fall into the trap of pretending to have it all together.

What are the greatest things you have seen God do related to the revival in the last 20 years?

Some of the most amazing things I saw related to the revival happened within the first six months. The ten and a half hour service at Wheaton College in March of 1995 is still one of the most powerful services I've ever attended. About a week after graduating that May, Susan and I were invited to speak in three churches in three different states over three weeks. The trip extended to nine weeks, and we spoke 54 times. A year later Susan and I started dating and several years later we were married. We still talk about those revival days and how we saw marriages healed, families restored, and learned to trust the Lord to provide for needs. Now as we interact with the persecuted church we regularly meet people who have gone or will go to prison for their faith, who risk so much to live out their faith. But even for them we stress the need of staying close to the Lord, having accountability, and trusting the Lord to provide all needs.

Is there anything else you would like people to know about the revival or its affect in your life?

Over the years I've heard people talk about how much they desire revival in their life, their church, or their community. However, much of the time I think people want to jump to the good things (restored relationships, healed marriages, youth turning back their hearts) without dealing with serious sin in their life. What we saw 20 years ago and still see today is that there isn't a formula for revival and there are no shortcuts. It comes down to God doing supernatural things. However, biblically we see that the key components are still prayer, taking sin seriously, confessing, repenting, and trusting God to then do things only He can do. 2 Chronicles 7:14 still rings true, "If my people who are called by name humble themselves, and pray and seek my face and turn from their wicked ways, then I will hear from heaven and will forgive their sin and heal their land."

What are pertinent positions and life experiences that would help us know more about your life since the days of the revival?

Susan and I have lived overseas the past 12 years trying to be a light for the Lord. We have been given the opportunity to share Truth in over 10 countries and shared with countless people from varying locations and religious backgrounds since the revival. We currently live in the Middle East with our four children.

MARTY MCGUKIN

Now 20 years later, what means the most to you about the revival?

More than anything I am thankful that God did not let revival happen only in me. There are many friends, I call family, who speak this language, they know, like I know, that good music does not equal the presence of God. They know that the hand and power of God are real. They know the stories, they remember the same images. They too long for a greater grip of Christ than just the hem of the garment to which we desperately clung. They know these things and when waves of grief wash over me, they remind me. They strengthen my heart. Those who have walked this road are the ones who understand the valley of the shadow for they too have died to themselves. I am not alone. That gives me strength to minister when its not so easy.

How does the revival affect your life now?

There has been and I suppose will always be a gnawing hope of seeing a movement of God with such power again. I recently was doing some design work and ran across this quote by Oliver Wendell Holmes: "A mind that is stretched by a new experience can never go back to its old dimensions." The last four years have been filled with unspeakable grief at the loss of my parents after a deadly car crash. Oftentimes well meaning individuals would tell me how my parents were looking down on me. I would receive cards about how the rainbow was my mother saying hello or my dad seeking to help me heal. Oh how I have deeply longed for the temporary comfort that bad theology brings. But, I know the heart of God. I have seen Him, unmistakably, in action. The reality of who God is and how he interacts with His children is burned into my brain—images of us weeping before him on the altars of the churches where His hand fell mightily. So when someone says my parents are looking down on me, I quickly tell them that yes my parents are looking down, only because they are bowed before my God in heaven. That is a healing and a peace easy theology cannot bring. That faith comes only from being hidden in the cleft of the rock as the Almighty passes by—and all that I am, all that I have, all that I thought my life would be—dies. We cannot see God and live. Revival has brought a continual death to me. And the life it brings is not my own, but His, full of peace or purpose and the assurance of heaven.

What are the greatest things you have seen God do related to the revival in the last 20 years?

I told my husband of all that happened as best I could. He, a pastor, would smile and nod, not ever fully understanding. Then God began to get to his heart. One day he came home carrying Henry Blackaby's book *Holiness*. He had tears in his eyes. He looked at me and said, "So it was real? Everything you said was real!" Shortly after that we began to work through that book and the first book released by you guys with our college ministry. We grew from about 24 to 300. Our heart was to continue this ministry in Wilmington, but our current pastor thought it was best that we leave. So, we sold everything we had and began to travel around the nation speaking to college students about revival and spiritual awakening. God did not come down in thunder to any of the "meetings" we held. He did however use us to challenge many students to look deeper at who God was.

My marriage has never been the same since. Every church where my husband has served has been challenged with the truths of revival and spiritual awakening. We will never go back to our old dimensions.

Is there anything else you would like people to know about the revival or its affect in your life?

When God changed the heart of my husband, I felt like I was finally able to express who I was at the core of my faith in Christ. We are not mega church leaders, nor do we want to be. We have adopted two special needs children who both were on dialysis. Graciously, I have learned more about kidneys than I ever thought possible. We have been able to touch many lives with the gospel, including the birth parents of our youngest son who live in communist China. They worship God in an underground church there.

Recently we felt called of God to move to the mission field. We always wanted to live in Africa. We even went to Botswana and talked to the students at the University of Botswana about revival and spiritual awakening and prayed God would release us to move there. His answer was no. Shortly after we returned He moved us to Alabama where we adopted the two children on dialysis. We knew we were doing what God had called us to do, but we also knew our family of three who deeply wanted to serve as foreign missionaries, would never be commissioned with the needs our new children had. Last year God began to stir our hearts to go to the mission field. We were a little puzzled. He redirected our understanding. Matt now serves as a pastor in Idaho. The city we live in is about 90% Mormon. Talk about a mission field! And, our children transferred their medical care to Salt Lake City (our youngest received a transplant right before we moved). Now we have an even greater opportunity to speak the truth of the gospel into the lives of more medical personnel.

What are pertinent positions and life experiences that would help us know more about your life since the days of the revival?

I am a stay at home mom—no time to work when you have two kids on dialysis! I am just an ordinary, nothing special kind of gal living a normal, yet God-infused life. I am excited to say I was able to lead a lady who was baptized into the Mormon church to Christ recently and have begun one-on-one discipleship with her. Her son, also not a believer, is in my son's class and football team. God has given my Micah a heart to see him come to know the Lord. That is one of the greatest blessings of seeing God move—seeing Him move in your kids to prompt them to share the Gospel with others.

KELLY AND BRANDI PARRISH

Now 20 years later, what means the most to you about the revival?

There are a couple of things that still mean so much to us. One is the way that we saw God move—the healing He brought and the miracles that He performed. We often talk about how it stretched our faith and how we want so badly for our own kids to see God move in big ways like that. We pray now believing that God really will bring revival again because we have seen with our very own eyes. We are hungry to always see God move powerfully again and cannot settle for mediocrity. The second thing that means so much to us is that that time was the beginning of us saying "Yes" to Jesus, no matter what. It was the start of a journey that put us in many places of leadership and has ultimately led us to become church planters.

How does the revival affect your life now?

We want to see Jesus. We want to see Him do big things and we want to be apart of it! We pray BIG prayers. We pray a lot. We believe that God will do what He promises. We see His faithfulness. We also remember the fear that came with agreeing to share our story and still deal with that fear today. The revival put sight to our faith and those visions were so powerful that they still vividly remain. We can fight through our fears knowing that God answers our prayers, because we have seen Him do it.

What are the greatest things you have seen God do related to the revival in the last 20 years?

God has given us opportunities to keep telling the story—our story—and it is always powerful. Being able to talk about Jesus and the things He has done in our lives never gets old or loses power. We have seen people come to Christ because we have shared with them how God loved us even though we were sinners and how He has used us to bring Him glory. On a personal level, being able to believe God for things in our lives has come because of seeing His faithfulness at such a young age. We have been able to experience God in big ways and follow Him in obedience. We believe that because of our involvement in the revival, that God has brought us to Northern Colorado to share the gospel with the unreached because we want so badly for them to see and experience Jesus in the ways that we have. The reality that so many people do not know Jesus and live their lives without experiencing His healing power, love, grace and mercy stops us in our tracks. We saw God bring healing to our own lives and experienced freedom from sins that had us in bondage. We have dedicated our lives to sharing that freedom and gift with others.

Is there anything else you would like people to know about the revival or its affect in your life?

We learned a very powerful lesson of following the leadership of the Holy Spirit during the revival. It was when we gave Him the freedom to work that we saw Him move in mighty ways. This has had a profound impact on our lives as we have pursued and followed after Jesus. We haven't had to be bound by rules and regulations of "this is what it should look like" or "this is how things are supposed to happen." There has been freedom in giving the Holy Spirit free reign to mold, make, guide and direct our lives. We haven't always done things like everyone else because we have believed that when we are walking with God and allowing Him freedom in our lives, His plan is always bigger and better than ours.

What are pertinent positions and life experiences that would help us know more about your life since the days of the revival?

Kelly: I served in lay leadership in every church we attended, including as a deacon, Sunday School teacher, on Missions Committees, Men's Bible Study leader, and numerous other positions. After teaching and coaching for 10 years, I went to work in the oil and gas industry. Five years ago I surrendered to full-time ministry and began the training for church planting. Currently, I'm the Lead Pastor of Living Rock Church in Fort Collins,

Colorado. I'm a LAUNCH Network and NAMB Church Planter and I'm frequently asked to share of the successes God is granting through walking in His faithfulness.

Brandi: I've also served in lay leadership teaching couples and Women's Bible studies. I've written several Bible studies and speak at Women's events and conferences. I currently serve beside Kelly as a Church Planters Wife.

We both serve every year at the Passion Conference in Atlanta as Community Group Leaders. God did such a work in our lives during our college years that we love serving students. We also try to always have college students in our lives that we are personally discipling in hopes that they may experience Jesus in ways that we have.

DOUG MUNTON, PASTOR AT FIRST BAPTIST, CORINTH, TEXAS IN 1995

Now 20 years later, what means the most to you about the revival?

I am so thankful God allowed me to see a taste of revival in my own life and church during this special time. I remember well taking a call from John Avant one night 20 years ago when I was pastor at FBC Corinth. He told me what God was doing in Brownwood. My soul thrilled at the testimony of revival. After the call, I got down on my knees and just poured out my heart to God, asking Him to do a work in my own heart. I contacted a couple of the Howard Payne students and asked them to come speak to our church on a Sunday night. Revival came that night and impacted my life and our church radically. It lasted for several weeks at our church. I was at Southwestern Baptist Seminary when revival came there. When I walked in the chapel I saw students praying and I felt the power of the Holy Spirit. I said to a friend, "God is here." I spoke with friends at my alma mater, Wheaton College, and encouraged them to have the Howard Payne students come. I spoke at several colleges (Criswell College being one) and several churches where revival came. The church where I have been pastor for the past 19 years now, First Baptist, O'Fallon, IL, experienced revival when John Avant came to speak at a conference for the state convention there. It is how I ended up coming to FBC O'Fallon.

How does the revival affect your life now?

I think of that time often as I know a little of what it is like to see God at work. It was such a sweet and powerful time and it has always left me longing for more. I still pray for revival. I can't be satisfied with spiritual mediocrity.

What are the greatest things you have seen God do related to the revival in the last 20 years?

God used it to deepen FBC Corinth, TX. That church was just spiritually vibrant. About a year after the revival, I left there to become the pastor at FBC O'Fallon, IL and the church was still vibrant long after I left. The revival really led to a strong start for me when I came FBC O'Fallon. The church grew tremendously as they were hungry for spiritual growth and God blessed and continues to bless this church.

Is there anything else you would like people to know about the revival or its affect in your life?

It has caused me to want more of God and not to be satisfied with going through the motions. It has caused me to long for a deep move of God again in my church and in our nation and world.

What are pertinent positions and life experiences that would help us know more about your life since the days of the revival?

I've continued to enjoy God's hand since those days. I left FBC Corinth, Texas, under the clear leadership of the Lord to come to FBC O'Fallon, Illinois in 1995, just one year after the time of revival. I've been here since that time as Senior Pastor. The church has more than tripled in size. I've been president of the Illinois Baptist State Association among other things. I've authored three books and contributed to several more. I am also an Adjunct Professor of Preaching and Evangelism at Liberty Baptist Theological Seminary.

TIM WILLIAMS

20 years later, what means the most to you about the revival?

The revival experience took an intellectual basis of knowing and relating to the Holy Spirit, out of that space, and changed my understanding of the freedom granting power He (the Holy Spirit) can and wants to grant to serious followers of Jesus Christ.

How does the revival affect your life now?

I still to this day, 20 years later, remember the hand of God touching me, and touching those at Howard Payne. I see the Holy Spirit minister around the things I do on a normal basis, giving opportunity to glorify and discuss Jesus.

What are the greatest things you have seen God do related to the revival in the last 20 years?

God exposed my heart to myself and excited others to seek the baptism of fire, seek revival, and to seek our heavenly Father more seriously.

Is there anything else you would like people to know about the revival or its affect in your life?

Revival itself is between you and our Heavenly Father. Of course, it can be experienced corporately. Also, the Lord does not want us to be focused on His previous movements and methods but rather on Him and what He is doing today!

What are pertinent positions and life experiences that would help us know more about your life since the days of the revival?

I was on staff at two churches as a youth minister, and on staff at Mission Arlington as a minister in many capacities. I'm a host and Bible teacher at my home. I also speak at my former church in a preaching capacity.

DONNA AVANT (WIFE TO JOHN)

Now 20 years later, what means the most to you about the revival?

My dad's salvation was a direct result of the Brownwood revival!

How does the revival affect your life now?

It is hard to do business as usual. It makes me frustrated with people who don't see big picture of all God can do.

What are the greatest things you have seen God do related to the revival in the last 20 years?

After praying for many years, to see my dad's salvation and the way it impacted the life of our family means the most.

Is there anything else you would like people to know about the revival or its affect in your life?

I'm just very humbled that the Lord allowed me to be a part of it!

TIM NAVRATIL

Now 20 years later, what means the most to you about the revival?

I remember the Brownwood revival with great fondness. God grabbed ahold of me at that time to fill me with a desire to serve him with all my life. That time was certainly a turning point in my life and in my marriage. Nancy and I were almost ready to separate due to my self-centeredness of that time. The weekend of the start of the revival we were at a weekend for couples in Dallas hosted by Henry and Marilynn Blackaby. God hit me over the head with a two-by-four that night and I wept like I had not wept for a long time as I saw how horribly self-centered I was. We drove home from the retreat to begin the week of revival meetings in Brownwood.

How does the revival affect your life now?

My cry to God at that time was, "Here am I, send me Lord." That is still the cry of my life today. I know that the Brownwood revival was a turning point in my spiritual life.

What are the greatest things you have seen God do related to the revival in the last 20 years?

I see what he has done in my life. I also keep up with Hector Dalton, as I know he was forever changed as well.

Is there anything else you would like people to know about the revival or its affect in your life?

God met many that week in a very powerful way, calling them to Himself as Lord.

What are pertinent positions and life experiences that would help us know more about your life since the days of the revival?

As a result of what God did during the revival as well as the work He continued to do years after, we sold our house and all our possessions and came to the mission field. Nancy and I have been in Asia for eight years now. I am a division level leader in Asia for ReachGlobal, the missionary arm of the Evangelical Free Church of America. Nancy and I live in Penang, Malaysia where we have lived for 2 ½ years now. Previously we lived in Wuhan, China.

CHRIS ROBESON

20 years later, what means the most to you about the revival?

The most significant impact of the 1995 revival in Brownwood upon my life is a continued challenge to be a faithful steward and herald of what God did to change lives for His glory. I was revived and so many others were revived to a new Biblical standard of the holiness of God and what He can do to set people free from the bondage of sin. The revival of 1995 is still something that impacts and motivates me today to seek the Lord for His glory to be at work in the world.

How does the revival affect your life now?

The revival impacts my life today as a believer and as

a pastor. As a fellow believer, I pray that revival comes to our nation and the nations of the world. As a pastor, I pray that I am sensitive to what God may want to accomplish in any given worship service that may be "unplanned" and "spontaneous" while remaining grounded in Biblical precepts and principles that are appropriate for God's people.

There remains a longing for the glory of God to be poured out again and to experience new and fresh encounters with the Lord in His holiness. This is an abiding burden that remains in my heart as a result of having tasted and seen so much of what God can do supernaturally. Revival ministry is a uniquely set apart ministry. Some people aren't interested or simply don't see the need for revival. My life has been genuinely ruined for the glory of God. I am ruined in the sense that I'm never content just to play church or to allow those around me to settle for less of God. I'm not trying to recreate a Brownwood Revival, but I am trying to share with people that there is more of God that's available if we will surrender all things to Him.

What are the greatest things you have seen God do related to the revival in the last 20 years?

I am humbled and amazed at how God still uses the story of revival at Coggin Ave. Baptist Church and so many college campuses to encourage other pastors and believers to begin praying and asking God to bring revival in their lives, their church, and on their campuses. Stories of people encountering God are always powerful as these encounters lead to people being changed forever for the glory of God.

Is there anything else you would like people to know

about the revival or its affect in your life?

During the revival itself, there were those who questioned the authenticity of the services and whether or not such "confession" services were appropriate. Some said that we shouldn't call what we were experiencing as an actual revival until some time had passed. I guess twenty years will suffice and I can honestly say that if anyone has a better word than revival for what we experienced together, let me know, I'll be glad to call it that instead! As for me, I was revived to the glory of God and I continue to be revived by having a hunger for seeing God's glory at work and I contribute this longing to my personal experience in Brownwood, both at church at Coggin Ave. and on the college campus at Howard Payne University.

What are pertinent positions and life experiences that would help us know more about your life since the days of the revival?

I have walked with the Lord since those days and continue to serve as a pastor of a Southern Baptist Church in Texas.

We want to add two final testimonies from those days. The first relates to a place mentioned briefly earlier regarding a college campus and student leaders not directly related to the Brownwood revival, but definitely a part of what God was doing and what He continues to do. I (Alvin) moved my family to Wake Forest, North Carolina, in August 1995 to teach at Southeastern Baptist Theological Seminary. As I began teaching, I could not help but tell my students about what I had seen in Houston that spring. A young man fresh out of college spoke to me about a Bible study he had started at his alma mater, a school about an hour and a half away. He asked me to speak to the group, and off we went on a Monday night.

I spoke to between 100-200 students outside a campus building. I sensed the same presence of God I had seen in Houston! After speaking, God began to convict students. They continued to pray and share with one another until after 1:00 AM, when I returned to campus with my student. I learned later of students who surrendered to missions that night, and of at least one backslidden student who surrendered his life to Jesus and later became a student pastor, among others.

I learned the next day that a senior leader of the group made a bonfire that night where students, not unlike what happened at Wheaton with garbage bags, brought things that hindered their walk with Christ to burn them.

The student who brought me and the senior leader that night both became students of mine and led a ministry focusing on revival among college students for a season. We have remained close friends. God has used them greatly in my life and the lives of many. The new SEBTS student? J.D. Greear, now lead pastor of the Summit Church in Raleigh Durham, one of the most effective churches in America at reaching the next generation. The senior leader's name? Bruce Ashford, now Provost at Southeastern.

Revival raises up a generation of leaders.

This final one is not a twenty-year later update, but offers a beautiful picture of what happens in revival. Perhaps you remember the story of the fifteen-year-old pregnant girl at Jersey Village Baptist Church? I (Alvin) never met her that night personally, but he did hear later how she and her family decided to give the baby up for adoption. Some eight years later, in 2003, I got this email on a Thursday morning in my office at Southeastern Seminary:

Dr. Reid:

> I am not sure if you remember me, but I was the fifteen-year-old pregnant girl. I wanted to let you know that I recently sought out a copy of [the original *Revival* book] and began to read it for the first time in many years, and the passage about me brought me to tears. I wanted to thank you for putting my story in there . . . . I was glad to read something done entirely by a stranger and get an outside perspective of that situation after [finding] healing. I would love if that passage in some, even small way helped another person, but just for myself it was nice to remember some of the details that I had forgotten.

> I also wanted to give you an update on me. I recently graduated [from college] and am married to the most wonderful man I have ever known. I am planning on going to medical school and becoming a pediatrician.

> I placed my two-day-old son for adoption . . . . He is a wonderful, almost eight-year-old, stubborn boy. His parents are wonderful and I am truly blessed to be allowed the chance to know him as he grows. He and his younger brother were ring bearers at my wedding. I could not imagine what my life would have been without him.

Marium

I sat and wept when I read this email. Then I called my wife, and then I immediately called John. It is impossible for me to say how many young people's lives have been touched by her story as I have spoken about revival in my classes and churches. This is the power of revival to change the trajectory of a life. May God let us see His good hand on a younger generation today.

CHAPTER 15
THINGS WE'VE LEARNED
THROUGH REVIVAL

JOHN AVANT

Revival revived... The word *revive* comes from two words –"re" which means "again," and "vive" which means "to live." So the basic meaning of the word is "to live again." Having experienced a movement where I saw the church I pastored, many other churches, more than 100 college campuses, and thousands of Christians fully "live again," I want to "live again" like that... again! That's revival revived. That's why we are writing this book. We long for a fresh movement of God. We can still taste what it was like. We can still hear the cries to God. We can still see the tears. But we don't want to taste, see and hear it all again only in our memories. We want and need revival. For our own lives. But our desire for revival is not selfish nostalgia. History rises up before us and cries out that revival is the only real hope for a nation. The concept of revival is rooted in the Scriptures where we see nation-saving movements of God under the leadership of men like Hezekiah and Nehemiah. But the word *revival* itself was not used in English in a spiritual sense until Cotton Mather called for *revival* in 1702 in his work *Magnalia Christi Americana*. Since then the word and the movements the word describes have come to be central to the spiritual history of our nation as well as others.

Once again it appears clear that the future of

America and indeed the world hinges upon a fresh awakening—a revival grounded in the Gospel and expressed uniquely in contemporary culture. This is what we pray for—what we thirst for!

But it is important to note that revival is not *first* about changing the culture or even reaching the lost. It is always first and foremost about God and God's people. Revival happens when the Church begins to *live again* as she is meant to. Then this leads to the kind of proclamation, evangelism and transformation that impacts the unreached world with the gospel. "But you are a chosen race, a royal priesthood, a holy nation, a people for his own possession, *that you may proclaim* the excellencies of him who called you out of darkness into his marvelous light." 1 Peter 2:9 (ESV)

Revival is simply the Church living fully as the Church!

This is immensely important to understand. When we hear people praying for revival, we wonder if they have even thought about what they are praying for! Revival is not a service or a series of services (though that is the definition *Dictionary.com* gives for the word!) Revival is not spiritual fervor though passion and fervor are definitely present when God moves. Revival is not a particular set of phenomena. Revival is not evangelism, though it always leads to it. And revival is certainly not a return of "the good old days," which invariably means "*my* days!" I once heard a woman say that she was praying for a revival of "old-fashioned music." I asked her if she meant the Gregorian Chants! Her eyes glazed over. I explained to her that those chants were definitely old-fashioned. It quickly became evident that she was only concerned with music she personally liked from *her* day.

Revival is not about affirming our preferences in worship or church life.

Revival is not about our preferences at all. It is about the glory of God displayed fully in His Church. And so we are afraid that many who pray for revival will not like it at all if it comes! For it is guaranteed to bring massive change, to be quite uncomfortable, and to propel the Church into the future not the past.

So when we say we are praying for revival, let's be clear and specific about what we are praying for.

We are praying for the Spirit of God to move and for His people to respond to Him in such a way that the Church *lives again* fully as she is meant to.

Whenever this has occurred the changes both to the Church and to its surrounding culture are profound and wonderful. Apart from revival a church begins to look like something less than a church. Something other than a church. A religious club maybe. Perhaps a high-energy show. Or a low-energy funeral. But something other than what the Church is meant to be and can be.

I have dear friends who recently moved to a different city and began the process of finding a church home. They had dearly loved their church and had been a part of it for years so this was a somewhat painful and challenging process. When they found the church they believed God had led them to they went to a room where nice people met them and asked them to fill out some information. Their highly suspicious young son spoke up loudly for all to hear and said, "Mom, Dad, before we sign anything check this out to be sure this is not a scam!"

Unfortunately the average church in America today exists as something of a scam. We claim to be a people wholly given over to the glory of God and the advancement of His kingdom. But in reality we appear to be more about our own likes and dislikes, our own comfort, and the advancement of our own kingdoms.

Apart from revival, the Church is in danger of becoming a scam!

As we look back on the movement known as the Brownwood revival and reflect on what we have learned from it and through it, we hope that we can make some observations that will help your church and ours to truly be the church, to live again in health and vitality. And for all who come to share life with our churches to be in no danger of being scammed, but to find the authenticity and power of the Gospel.

We don't claim to be inerrant or comprehensive in these observations, but these two chapters reveal much of what we have learned through revival.

REVIVAL IS MYSTERIOUS

And that's a good thing! The Brownwood revival was scary and even threatening for some people. It didn't fit into our normal patterns of church life. We have never been able to fully answer the question of why revival came where it did, when it did, or to whom it did. It crossed over denominational lines. It affected people who believed significantly different doctrine than we did. In short, it was mysterious. Revival always is. It is the movement of the Creator of the Cosmos. Look at the pictures of the Cosmos from the Hubble telescope. Wow! The beauty. The grandeur. The mystery! How could anything that flows from this all-encompassing King not be mysterious?

We believe that one of the least understood reasons

for the lack of revival in the church today is the failure of God's people to embrace mystery as a part of God's good plan for us. We tend to want all the points of our theological systems to exist in the realm of "black and white"—if someone disagrees then we create walls between them and us. Revival never happens until walls come down! We want our ecclesiological preferences to be black and white as well. My way of worship or church structure is right. When others disagree divisive walls are built brick by brick. The divisions in our churches are lethal to revival! Revival will not happen until these walls come down.

So what if embracing mystery is actually a really good thing? In fact what if it is God's will and the path that can lead us to unity and a fresh movement of God among us? What if we can't even fully *know* God without abandoning our certainties and embracing his mysteries?

What if God, and revival, is gray? Or grey?

Huh?

Bear with me for a while and we will see if we can make this mysteriously clear!

The blend of breath-taking beauty and pervasive lostness was overpowering. Sitting in the shadow of medieval castles and majestic mountains, on the banks of the Neckar River, Gary and I sipped our frappuccinos as we watched the people stream by. We had met up in Heidelberg to spend some time together letting the call of the gospel challenge our souls. Everyone needs someone in their lives who loves them but always speaks truth and a challenge from the heart of God. Gary is that person to me. He lives in Germany where his mission work is based. Germany has recently been called "the most godless place on earth."[1] Especially in the eastern part of

Germany, surveys show that about half the population is atheist and among those under 28 years old, 71% have never believed in the existence of God.

"Look at all of them John. If the statistics are even close, few if any of these people know Jesus. They don't even know *how* to know him! What is the church doing about it? Not much. Most churches are not doing much about the lostness right under their noses."

"I know. What's the answer, Gary?" I asked.

"Well it has to start with us, that's for sure. What will *you* do about it John? You speak to a lot of people. You write books. That's good but it's dangerous too. It could subtly become all about you. What mountain are you climbing John? Are you climbing Mt. John or one worth climbing? On the day of my death, whether by bullets or old age, I want there to be no question that my mountain to climb was to take the gospel to the hardest places on earth… and kick the devil's a**!"

I didn't speak after that for quite some time.

Now before you get all judgmental that Gary used a bad word, let me ask you a question.

How mad would *you* be at the devil if you saw your own wife gunned down on the mission field by a terrorist for the sake of the gospel?

Gary Witherall's wife Bonnie was murdered in southern Lebanon in 2002.

Does it strike you as amazing that Gary is mad at the devil instead of God? After all, doesn't his wife's murder raise some pretty disturbing questions about God? Did He plan and will Bonnie to be shot to death in cold blood? If so, what does that say about the character of God? How can a God of love will such horror for his children? Especially a missionary. A woman giving herself away for others. If God did not will it how can He still be sovereign? Are we subject to every accident and evil that happens around us each day? Is God just an observer?

And yet with all these questions and more before him night and day, in the midst of unspeakable grief and crushing loss, Gary ran *to* God not away from Him, even when the questions weren't answered. Gary centered his passion in the gospel and focused his fury on the enemy. When you are with him, you want to put your foot beside his and kick the devil's a** too!

How did Gary come through death and darkness and arrive at a wonderful place, re-married to a great woman with four beautiful children, reaching out as a missionary to the same people who murdered his wife? What makes him different from believers who go through terrible suffering and end up bitter and angry?

Gary embraced mystery. Gary embraces a mysterious God.

And that God and His many mysteries has healed him and freed him.

And that's what revival is ultimately about: how to be set free by mystery.

Free from all that boils inside and hinders you. Free *to* all God intends for you to be. Free to share the mystery of God with others in a movement called a church. A church revived as she is meant to be. Free. Freed by mystery. How can that be?

Well first we will have to admit that Gary was right about something else: we all tend to climb our own mountain. I know I do. I can be a fully committed climber of Mt. John. But that never works out well. My self-centeredness always leaves me, well, centered in self. And there's nothing in self that fulfills in the least. But my problem is I want to be the center. I want to be right. I want to win the argument. I want to have everything figured out. And I want everyone to know I have everything figured out.

And when I function that way I am helping ensure that revival continues to be hindered!

Part of that is my own insecurity. Another part of it is my desire to defend God. If I can't answer all the questions about Him and put it all in a neat package that is palatable to even those that don't know Him yet, maybe people won't believe in Him.

But the truth is that God really doesn't need me to help him out. He is not interested in my efforts to solve all His mysteries. In fact, He wants me to embrace His mysteries as a key to freedom.

1 Timothy 3:16 says: "Beyond all question, the mystery of godliness is great: He appeared in a body, was vindicated by the Spirit, was seen by angels, was preached among the nations, was believed on in the world, was taken up in glory."

The Word of God says that there is no question at all that His mysteries are *great*. Not just good. They are great even in God's eyes. They are to be embraced. Scholars agree that this verse was actually sung as a hymn of the early church. They even sang the mysteries of God!

Who can explain all the things those verses mentioned? Who can articulate everything about the incarnation, all that it means? We don't have to *get* it all to believe it all. 1 Corinthians 15:51 says that the most important thing in all of our lives, our eternity, is fraught with mystery: "Listen I tell you a mystery: We will not all sleep, but we will all be changed."

There is more mystery there than I can even comprehend! What if we have missed the joy of mystery while we are busy trying to form correct doctrine and defend our faith? What if that is a key reason why revival is hindered?

Can we be biblical and yet not see *everything* as black and white?

A Gray Square

Or is it? Now this doesn't seem too complex. That picture is a gray colored square. Right? Right.

Are you sure?

Are you sure it is not a *grey* square? Cloford.com is perhaps the most authoritative resource on color swatches. They indicate that the square would have to be darker to be *gray*. More like this:

Most dictionaries disagree however and affirm that both spellings are correct for the same color. *Grey* is used more commonly in Great Britain and *gray* is the correct spelling in America. Evidence for this comes from *Webster's Academic Dictionary,* an American dictionary from 1867, where the entry for *grey* refers the reader to *gray.* However, this view is problematic too since the preeminent *British* lexicographer Samuel Johnson argued that *gray* was the correct spelling. But even though he wrote the *Dictionary of the English Language* in 1755, which was the authoritative British dictionary for 150 years, he lost the gray versus grey battle. *Grey* became the recognized spelling of the word in Great Britain. After years of fighting this injustice, he died a broken man on a cold *gray* English morn. Okay, I made that part up. There's no evidence that it bothered him all that much.

So which is it? A *gray* colored square or a *grey* colored square? Maybe that's not even the right question. If we go back to cloford.com they don't list either gray *or* grey as colors. They are *colours.* Either spelling of that word is correct as well.

Head spinning yet? Why you may ask, am I laboring so intricately through all this. Or *labouring.*

Because words matter. How we use them and what they mean matter. Words start romances that produce generations. Words start wars that destroy generations. Words start great spiritual movements that shape history. Words spoken at Coggin Avenue Baptist Church and Howard Payne University by a few students launched the Brownwood revival. Words split and even destroy churches that were not meant to be destroyed by even hell itself. The right words at the right moment can lift a person from despair to hope. The wrong words at the wrong moment can leave scars for life that destroy hope.

G.F. Northall, in 1894 was the first to print the children's rhyme "Sticks and stones will break my bones but words will never hurt me." He was an idiot. (He's not alive to be offended by that but words apparently wouldn't have hurt him anyway.) Words hurt terribly and words heal wonderfully.

Words *really* matter.

And for those of us who follow Jesus, we have staked everything on the One who came to this world as the Word made flesh (John 1:14) and who will come again to this world as the Word of God. (Revelation 19:13)

As Jesus-followers we believe his words. We believe *the* Word. We believe that "All Scripture is God-breathed and is useful for teaching, rebuking, correcting and training in righteousness." (2 Timothy 3:16) We believe that the Word, his words, are powerful to sustain us, to direct us, and to change us. They are "living and active, sharper than any double-edged sword..." (Hebrews 4:12)

This is not a book written to defend the truth of Scripture. We believe the Bible. If you doubt its truth there are great books to defend its reliability. That is not the purpose of this book. But it is important for you to know that we believe it. Every word of it. Because we are calling into question not the truth of the Bible, but how we *approach* its truth. Because if we mess that up...

We will become the people who killed Jesus!

How can I say something that strong? Because we have a very good historical record of the people who hated Jesus and had him killed. And shockingly, no one believed the Bible more than they did! The Pharisees were passionate about the truth of the law. But their fundamental distinction was that they kept *adding* their own interpretation to it until it was hard to distinguish between the words of God and the words of men. Their passion not for the Word, but for *their understanding* of it led them to the depths of human evil. And Pilate was no better. Having heard and seen Truth standing before him and even being warned by his wife to leave Jesus alone, he asks him "What is truth?" (John18:38) and sends Truth to the cross.

The Pharisees approached truth with legalism; Pilate with skepticism. The result was the same.

And it still is.

We are the *Body of Christ.* So when we attack each other over our differing understanding of the Scriptures, we are ripping and clawing at the flesh of the Lord. His body. We are killing Jesus again. The same One who prayed that somehow, despite all our differences, "all of them may be one Father, just as you are in me and I am in you..." (John 17:21)

So let's give Jesus a break. Let's give ourselves a break. If we insist on carrying on our own version of the gray/grey debate, certain that we must not only answer every tough question of life for ourselves, but also convince everyone else that *our* gray is right and their *grey* is wrong, what will the results be?

We will become angry and arrogant people. We will split the body of Christ that He longs to revive. We will miss the joy and freedom that is meant to be our inheritance. We will never experience revival!

In our efforts to make everything black or white... *we will miss God's gray!*

So we want to propose something different. Something risky and radical. Something adventurous and transformational. Something wildly liberating.

Abandon our prideful need to be right and embrace the wonder of the mystery of God!

This is not a book primarily about theology. It is a book about living in joy and joyful relationships. It is a book about revival in the past and contemporary revival in the Church today. And about not missing the best parts of God and His Word: the mysterious parts. The parts that are hard to understand. The parts we fight about. This is a book about living the life we were meant to live now while taking incredibly seriously the life forever for which we are being shaped.

So how do we live this life?

We will have to go Gray!

Think about what gray really is. It is black *and* white. It cannot be black *or* white. All my life I have heard evangelicals bemoaning "gray areas." Everything is supposed to be black or white. One way or the other, gray is compromise.

But what if much of life is gray?

What if in our efforts to understand everything correctly we have missed the blend of God? What if we are *meant* to embrace positions in the bible and in life that *seem* to be contradictory?

Now, I'm not talking about relativism.

Remember we have just made it clear that we believe the Bible. But do *we really* believe it? Or do we often create our own systems and "isms" in an effort to have it all make perfect, logical sense.

What if the Bible is often gray?

Going gray does not mean believing less of the Bible It means believing that God is more than we have made Him out to be. Bigger than our petty arguments about

Him. He can be black *and* white. At the same time. He is God. And He can be gray. Going gray is living in the big, giant, amazing mystery of God. And there's nothing like that life! It is a life of faith. And faith doesn't give us everything in clean, neat black and white. Faith always has a gray side to it.

Remember our "gray/grey" lexicographer Samuel Johnson? He once said, "No people can be great who have ceased to be virtuous."

I want to live a great life, don't you? I only get one of them here on this earth. We fear that much of the people called the Church have ceased to be virtuous. Not just because of all the statistics we have heard so many times about divorce and sexual sin and all the other ways we are messing up life. But because we are becoming too much like the Pharisees. Or Pilate. Take your pick.

We want to go on a journey to be like Jesus. The One who embraced all the mystery of the Incarnation and "for the *joy* set before him endured the cross." (Hebrews 12:2) We want in on that joy. So we need in on that mystery.

We need to go gray.

On the surface, gray doesn't seem like much of a color. Not very attractive. KMB Designs says "Gray is neutral, non-committal, cold, sophisticated. Grey (yes they use both spellings!) can also signify gloominess, sadness, ghosts, ashes, cobwebs, and the dust of a haunted house and other scary things. People who like grey tend to be neutral about life. They like to protect themselves from the hectic world in a blanket of non-commitment preferring a secure, safe, balanced existence."

Yuk. Not the life we want to live. But what if even the color gray is not black or white? The website

Sensational Colors which discusses the psychology of color has another take on gray. They say that the color gray affects us physically by unsettling us and creating expectations. Now that's more like it.

And those slightly odd Feng Shui folks say that "grey can be used to initiate a process that transforms thought into action."

Now we're talking!

And best of all is the Herder Dictionary of Symbols: "Grey consists equally of black and white. It is the color of mediation and compensating justice…in Christianity it is the color of the resurrection of the dead…"

That's the gray we want to be! Color the Church a resurrected revival shade of gray, Lord!

So back to the gray square. Could it be alright for it to be both gray and grey, both a color and a colour? Could it be alright for life to be like that? In fact if we were to find a lot of greyness in the Bible itself could it be that going gray could really set us free? Let's find out. Let's go after the gray. We will find there is a lot of mystery to embrace. And just maybe a lot of revival to experience if we don't' have to have it in our neat, tidy package.

And oh by the way, the gray square isn't. A square that is. Measure it for yourself.

REVIVAL REQUIRES HUMAN LEADERSHIP

This is not to say that God could not bring revival without utilizing human leaders. He is God and can do as He pleases. But thus far He has always used people, often the most unlikely people in the most unlikely places as stewards of the work of His Spirit. It is hard to conceive of the 1st Great Awakening without Jonathan Edwards, George Whitefield, John Wesley and so many others. Would there have been a great prayer revival in 1858 without a businessman named Jeremiah Lanphier? God used a 16 year-old girl named Florrie Evans to spark the Welsh revival and an eccentric preacher named Evan Roberts to lead it to its heights.

Sometimes the names don't become famous at all. Perhaps the most impactful part of the Brownwood revival did not take place in Brownwood at all but on the campus of Wheaton. There God used a couple of young, wide-eyed college students who shared their testimony.

From the pages of Scripture where we meet Ezra, Nehemiah, Hezekiah and others to the history of revival in the Church since then, we always find someone who God chooses to use when He is ready to move. He works long before revival takes place to prepare the lives of those He intends to use. Had it not been for wise counsel and even gentle rebuke from men like Henry Blackaby and Roy Fish, I would have never had my own personal repentance and revival season that led me to go to Brownwood. God may have used someone else instead but I would have missed out were it not for the influence of those leaders!

Henry Blackaby had been invited to Howard Payne long before the revival broke out. But he came at the perfect moment to give direction and leadership to the move of God among the students. God had His leader where He needed him when He needed him. This has intensified our passion to be fully available moment by moment to God's quiet call on our lives.

I think so very often about how different my life would be had I said no to a young student when he came forward and asked to share something with the church on January 22, 1995! What if I had been distracted by some petty thing? What if I had a fight with my wife that morning and just wasn't in the right spiritual place to hear God? In many ways revival has given me a deeper fear of God. The Bible talks a lot about the fear of the Lord. Having seen what God *can* do among his people, we fear missing what he *could* do in and through and around us if we are not prepared to hear his voice. The last time in the Bible where we are told to fear God is in Revelation 14:7 where it says, "Fear God and give him glory, because the hour of his judgment has come..." The verse is in the context of what appears to be a last great revival on the earth that leads to the fulfillment of the Great Commission. Verse 6 says, "Then I saw another angel flying directly overhead, with an eternal gospel to proclaim to those who dwell on the earth, to every nation and tribe and language and people." What if God, in the next year, or month, or week or minute desires to do something with us or with you that would allow us to be a part of this kind of revival before Jesus returns?! We fear missing that moment of opportunity. Revival has caused us to fear God more, to watch for Him more closely, to be ready to lead or serve, in whatever way He directs. Because we have also seen the results when leaders fail to join God in His work.

During the early days of the Brownwood revival I was

asked to go speak at a Baptist University and lead the students in a time of seeking God for revival. I flew in and spent the night in the hotel preparing my heart to speak to the student body. I knew the responsibility and the opportunity this represented as we were already seeing God do remarkable things on campuses around the country. The next morning I arrived with an expectant heart for what God might do that day. But as I walked in to speak, I was met by a rather embarrassed looking representative from the President's office who informed me that my chapel message had been cancelled! I was stunned. I asked if I could speak to the President to find out what his concerns were. He was not interested. I never got any kind of explanation. I heard later that there were concerns about "emotionalism," and also that I might be a "fundamentalist." Students were disappointed and confused. No one even seemed to know what I was supposed to do next or who was going to cover the expenses of my trip! To this day I find it one of the most cowardly and inexplicable things I have seen a Christian leader do.

I was preparing to make my way back to the airport and head home when word of the cancellation spread to another area school. The President there immediately asked me if I would be willing to change plans and speak there. I was grateful and we saw a wonderful move of God that day. But I have always wondered what might have been at the other school. Cancelling my speaking engagement was no big deal in itself. But for a leader to refuse to allow openness for God to move in fresh ways is a very big deal. So many had prepared and prayed. But one leader's decision stood in the way of the simple desire of students to hear of the mighty work of God and seek Him for themselves together.

Contrast this to the decision of another leader on the wonderful night of February 14, 1995, on the campus of Howard Payne University. God had begun to move powerfully after Henry Blackaby spoke. As we have recounted in this book, students had flooded to the altar, on their knees and faces before the Lord. Many were lined up to confess sin and to ask for prayer. The President of Howard Payne, Don Newbury, was in the audience that night. As revival began to break out I watched as Dr. Newbury stood up and began to walk forward. My heart was in my throat. What would he do? Would he take the microphone and put a stop to this? I watched in awe and respect as he simply walked to the altar, knelt and wrapped his arms around students who were crying out to God. He stayed there for a long time, just being present with students as God worked. His simple act of humility was actually a bold act of leadership. He offered personal credibility and support to what God was doing. I will never forget it. Without his leadership and support I have no doubt that the impact of the Brownwood revival would have been limited.

Two leaders. Two different responses. Unbelievably important lesson.

There is danger here though. Human leadership can easily morph into human arrogance. Though God seems to require human leadership when he moves powerfully, as soon as I think that *I* am required, I cease to be a leader God can use at all!

God is calling out leaders today who will lead with biblical balance—and who most importantly, will walk close enough with God to be able to hear *Him* lead *us*! When God begins to move in a unique and surprising way there is no "revival manual" to help the leader know exactly what to do.

Should I let that student speak? Did that public confession of sin cross a line? Has this service gone on so long that people are losing focus on God? Is anything happening here that is not biblically grounded? Is any of the revival phenomena simply human emotion? Is there anything manipulative happening here? How do we turn this movement outward? How do we lead so that this movement is truly missional?

All these are actual questions we had to ask ourselves many times as we sought to carefully lead in the midst of revival. And notice that we are not really answering those questions in this book! We certainly learned a lot about these questions and some answers during the revival. But in reality there are no "one-size-fits-all" answers to these questions. We learned most of all that no matter how well we tried to know *what* to do, *who* we knew and how well we could hear him was far more important.

God uses human leaders in revival. Always. No exceptions that we can find. That is a wonderful possibility for all of us. He may well use you and me! But He's not waiting to see if you and I are great leaders. He's waiting to see if we are great lovers! If we love Him desperately. If we love His church desperately. If we love those he died for desperately. And yes, if we will change anything and everything needed in our churches so that His desperately needed revival may come. Then just maybe we will see Him move again in revival.

If we are tempted toward pride as leaders God always has his way of taking us down a notch or two. I was preaching overseas. A man came up afterwards with a copy of my book *Authentic Power*. He asked me to sign it. As I did he proceeded to tell me how much my writing had meant to him in the past and how he couldn't wait to read this book and how amazed he was to meet me personally. I was feeling pretty good about myself until as he started to walk away he said, "I just can't believe I got to meet John *Piper* face to face!"

Keep us humble God but use us!

REVIVAL FLOWS THROUGH THE YOUNG AND THE YOUNG AT HEART

Six hundred years before the birth of Christ God shocked a young teen with these words:

"Before I formed you in the womb I knew you, and before you were born I consecrated you, I appointed you a prophet to the nations." (Jeremiah 1:5)

A stunned young Jeremiah said, "Ah Lord God! Behold, I do not know how to speak, for I am only a youth." (Jeremiah 1:6)

Some Jewish writers place his age at no more than 14. The word *youth* is used in Hebrew of those still under the authority of their parents so it seems certain he was at least a teen. Hear God's response to Jeremiah's humble words: "Behold, I have put my words in your mouth. See, I have set you this day over nations and kingdoms, to pluck up and to break down, to destroy and to overthrow, to build and to plant." (Jeremiah 1:9, 10)

Clearly God, in His sovereign plan, uses the very young in movements that change whole nations and all of history! Some might question Jeremiah as a revival leader since God's people largely didn't listen to him and he witnessed the downfall of the whole nation. Jeremiah did see revival, though short-lived, under Josiah's reforms. But the real revival Jeremiah was a part of he never saw with human eyes but he did with the eyes of a prophet. In Chapter 29:10-14, Jeremiah sent a letter to the exiles in Babylon declaring to them that revival was coming!

> For thus says the Lord: When seventy years are completed in Babylon, *I will visit you*, and I will fulfill to you my promise and bring you back to this place. For I know the plans I have for you, declares the Lord, plans for welfare and not for evil, to give you a future and a hope. Then you will call upon me and come and pray to me, and I will hear you. You will seek me and find me, when you seek me with all your heart. I will be found by you, declares the Lord, and I will restore your fortunes and gather you from all the nations and all the places where I have driven you, declares the Lord, and I will bring you back to the place form which I sent you into exile.

It was young Jeremiah who announced the revival under Nehemiah!

Everywhere you find revival throughout history you will not have to look far to find the very young whom God is using. College campuses have long been fertile fields of revival: the Holy Club at Oxford in the 1700s, the Haystack Revival at Williams College and the Yale College Revival in the Second Great Awakening only scratch the surface of examples in the modern era.

As we look back on the Brownwood movement and all the places touched by that revival we see the continuation of this historic pattern. Of course at its heart the movement was a student revival. But there is another critical and related lesson we learned: revival flows most freely when the very young are supported, counseled and joined by those who are older yet young at heart!

When Chris Robeson stood and spoke at Coggin Avenue Baptist Church on January 22, 1995 an older woman immediately came and stood beside him and verbally affirmed his heart-cry for revival. During the early days of the revival at Coggin Avenue and many other churches, students' confession of sin was often intermingled with critical moments of brokenness among much older adults. One of the keys to the movement in Brownwood was reconciliation among older adults both in our church and also across racial lines in our city.

As the revival spread, students form Howard Payne and later other schools like Wheaton, went across the country sharing the mighty deeds of God. But so did older adults! We sent out schoolteachers, homemakers and our Chief of Police. Our Fire Chief actually became a missionary!

As God began to move among us, students were fasting and praying, sometimes all night. But long before that older adults were pouring out their hearts before God pleading for revival in our city. Pastors cried out to God together. Our prayer room had so many people praying there in those days that some of the prayer cards were completely black with the initials of those who had prayed. One of those was a card asking prayer for the salvation of my father-in-law, who miraculously came to Jesus. To this day we have kept that card.

Most significantly to me was an amazing man, now with Jesus, Carroll Lancaster, who came to me on the day of the revival's initial outbreak, and shared that God had spoken to him forty years before and called him to pray for revival at Coggin Avenue Baptist Church. He said, "Pastor for forty years I have rolled out of bed every day and onto my knees and prayed that God would revive our church today. And today is that day!"

Revival needs the energy and optimism of youth. But it also needs the wisdom and leadership of age—but only those who are young at heart—who have gotten older but have refused to "live old."

This could be one of the most important things we have learned from revival as it applies to the possibility of a fresh move of God in our day. What if older adults determined that the main purpose of the remainder of their days was not to enjoy the music they like or the preaching they enjoy, but to go like Abraham, in their later years where they have never been before–to encourage, mentor and support a young generation–and see a powerful and culture-changing revival again? More to say about this in the last chapter.

REVIVAL WILL EXTERNALIZE OR DE-MATERIALIZE

We often talk about the duration of revival movements. Historians discuss when the First Great Awakening began to wane or why the Jesus Movement was relatively short-lived. But these discussions are referring to the *phenomena* of revival. Authentic revival never ends! Jeremiah proclaimed that revival would come again to God's people. Nehemiah saw that revival happen. But we still reap the benefits because without a restored Jewish nation we would not have had a Jewish Savior come to all of us!

Every authentic revival is a missional movement. In recent decades we have seen "revivals" that largely consisted of big crowds of Christians participating in bizarre behavior that had little evangelistic impact, and in fact, often pushed the lost further away. Those movements, though dramatic, have had little long-term evangelistic impact.

Almost immediately the Brownwood revival began to externalize. Even before 1995 some of the students in our church had been a part of our mission work in Belarus. Several of us remembered later how a young man named Shawn Brown, during a powerful prayer meeting late one night in Belarus, prayed, "I just want to lay my life down before you Lord!" Later he did just that as one of those who was killed in the tragic shooting at Wedgewood Baptist Church.

Incredible numbers of people came to Christ in Brownwood as revived churches came together to share the gospel. And all over the world today are ministers and missionaries who have never been able to keep what God did in revival to themselves! We have already seen some of their stories in the previous chapter.

Revival is not for the purpose of making us happier in our church services. Revival is not first about us at all. Revival is about the display of the glory of God! And God is never more glorified than when the lost are saved. So why would God continue to bless any movement that becomes exclusive, territorial or internalized? Authentic revival always has and always will propel us into the Great Commission!

Selfishly the greatest thing we have learned from revival is how much we personally needed it! And still do. We can never be the same because of what we witnessed and experienced. We don't want to be the same! Once you have been truly "in love" it is hard to imagine being "out of love." Revival is God's great romance. To have it and lose it feels something akin to divorce. We have not lost the personal impact of revival in both our lives. But our hearts break at the "divorce" of the Church from the movement of the Spirit in which the Church is meant to live—but from which she has departed. The Bride has deserted the Bridegroom. But He is waiting. And ready to take back His bride again. This is the revival we pray for and long for.

Notes:
1. Joe Carter, *Gospel Coalition,* 14 May 2012.

CHAPTER 16
THINGS WE'VE LEARNED
THROUGH REVIVAL

ALVIN L. REID

We can take hope in our time because our hope is in Christ, our reigning King. We also stand on the Scriptures which give us hope above our circumstances. In addition, we have history to encourage us. Over the past several centuries, great spiritual awakenings have touched the West, reviving believers, ushering multitudes into the church, planting churches, and launching missions movements globally.

In the late1600s a stagnant Lutheran church was set on fire by leaders like Philip Spener and A.H. Francke in the movement of Pietism. Spener's book *Pia Desideria*, the *Experiencing God* of his day if you will, called for ministers of the gospel in particular to follow Christ with radical obedience. Out of this movement the 100 year Moravian Prayer Movement was birthed.

In the early 1700s the American colonies had been settled by Europeans and had become spiritually dead. The First Great Awakening ignited the colonies, with leaders like Jonathan Edwards in New England, the Tennent family and Theodore Frelinghuysen in the middle colonies, and later through leaders like Baptists Shubal Stearns and Daniel Marshall. The movement was so powerful that secular historians like Perry Miller, long time professor at Harvard, argued that the Great Awakening did as much to shape the future nation called the United States as any factor. I would argue that Edwards' writings on revival are the most important documents outside of Scripture on the subject.

Around the same time God moved in Great Britain in an Evangelical Awakening led humanly by John and Charles Wesley, Howell Harris, and young George Whitefield. Whitefield also journeyed to the New World seven times and played a role in the revival fires in America.

Other movements followed such as the Second Great Awakening in the early 19th century, featuring church revival movements in the east and numerous college revivals, the frontier camp meetings west of the Appalachians, and the controversial ministry of Charles Finney. Finney's book *Revival Lectures* spread revival fire across the globe.

A Layman's Prayer Revival touched America in the late 1850s, while a powerful revival touched Wales at the same time. At the turn of the 20th century a Global Awakening recorded revival fires from the U.S. to Wales, from Japan to Australia, and from Africa to India. The 20th century witnessed numerous lesser movements in the United States, including seasons of college revivals in the 1950s, the Jesus Movement in the 1970s, and the Brownwood revival of 1995 considered here. The Pentecostal/Charismatic renewal has shaped global Christianity in the 20th century as much as any other movement.

To learn more about historic revival movements see Alvin L. Reid and Malcolm McDow, *Firefall 2.0.*

I've spent my life studying the events noted above. Here

are a few things I learned from those precious days in the early months of 1995, as well as a lifetime of study.

WHEN REVIVAL COMES, THE MOST RIGHTEOUS ARE THE MOST BROKEN

I have written seminary textbooks on revival. But when I was in the middle of one, I missed something very important, but something that has been obvious throughout this book. When revival comes, the most broken are the leaders. It was Isaiah, the most godly man in the nation, who was most broken over his own sin in Isaiah 6. Jonathan Edwards, although he had already witnessed powerful revival in his church, sat and wept as Whitefield preached in his church. The stories in these pages are not primarily the stories of the casual church attender, but of the most influential leaders who became broken over their own sin.

If you are a leader reading this, let me ask you a question: who is in your life who loves you but is not impressed by you, someone who can ask you hard questions and see when you blink? Leaders can isolate themselves into a position where they miss God at work.

WHEN REVIVAL COMES, EVANGELISM BECOMES A PASSION NOT A PROGRAM

Ideas spur movements. Osama Bin Laden helped to spawn a terrible movement of global terrorism at the turn of the 21st century by taking an extreme idea and convincing others to give their lives for it. Martin Luther did not seek to start a movement when he nailed the 95 theses to the wall, but a movement was born nevertheless because of the ideas he presented. The major movements in history, whether good or evil, grew and spread because of ideas, and typically, these ideas that challenged the status quo of the times. Revival movements bring the church back to the glory of Christ and the power of the gospel. As a result, evangelism programs become less necessary as evangelism activity naturally spreads from awakened believers.

Today, a growing movement of gospel recovery is spreading across the landscape of the church. This is particularly obvious in young adults. Weary of a factory-like church where attendees are basically expected to confess Jesus, show up every week at church services, and live morally, increasing numbers of young adults want to believe in something that changes everything. They hunger for a gospel recovery not unlike those we witnessed in earlier movements of God.

Tim Keller comments on why we need a focus on revival, and how the gospel is critical for such a movement:

> In other words, revivals and renewals are necessary because the default mode of the human heart is works-righteousness—we do not ordinarily live as if the gospel is true. Christians often believe in their heads that "Jesus accepts me; therefore I will live a good life," but their hearts and actions are functioning practically on the principle "I live a good life; therefore Jesus accepts me." The results of this inversion are smug self-satisfaction (if we feel we are living up to standards) or insecurity, anxiety, and self-hatred (if we feel we are failing to live up). In either case, the results are defensiveness, a critical spirit, and racial or cultural ethnocentricity to bolster a sense of righteousness, an allergy to change, and other forms of spiritual deadness, both individual and

corporate. In sharp contrast, the gospel of sheer grace offered to hopeless sinners will humble and comfort all at once. The results are joy, a willingness to admit faults, graciousness with all, and a lack of self-absorption.[1]

I believe that the wind of the Spirit is blowing in this gospel recovery, and I want to set my sails to that wind. So many people talk about revival as a form of behavior modification or as a means of putting a stamp on our current ministry practices instead of understanding it as a radical return to the gospel that leads to the remarkable surrender of lives for the purpose of living and sharing the mission of God.

WHEN REVIVAL COMES, PRAYER MATTERS MORE THAN EVER

Recently there was something of a twitter controversy over a prominent pastor who responded to a call to prayer for revival from the president of the Southern Baptist Convention. He tweeted, "Praying for revival equates to blaming God for the condition of your local church." When he was challenged by another pastor he responded, "Your church is great because it's led well, not because your church is praying and waiting for revival."

Now I understood what he was getting at and to an extent I agree—he was saying that many churches refuse to make the changes that God would have them to make to reach lost and unchurched people. They resist change and cling to preference and tradition, and simply call for revival, which for them means God's endorsement on their refusal to change. They are indeed hindering many churches from revival. But the inference of the tweets nonetheless is dangerously man-centered. When one of America's largest churches says that churches are great because they are led well it gives too much credit to a pastor and not enough to the glory of God. Isaiah 48:11 says, "For my own sake, for my own sake I do it, for how should my name be profaned? My glory I will not give to another." I have been told that Billy Graham keeps a plaque on his desk that says, "Touch not the glory…" A great reminder to all of us called to lead God's people toward movements of God. God will use me. He may even choose to use me greatly. But it is never *about* me!

When revival comes, prayer becomes a passion not a pastime. How should we pray for revival?

1. *If we simply use prayer for revival as an excuse for our unwillingness to obey God, we should not pray for revival, we should repent.* Prayer for revival is not a band aid cure; it is a call to repentance. If we are not passionate about sharing the gospel, honoring the Word, and bringing glory to God, our prayers for revival are meaningless. Note the words of Tozer: *"Have you noticed how much praying for revival has been going on of late–and how little revival has resulted? I believe the problem is that we have been trying to substitute praying for obeying, and it simply will not work."*

2. *If we see revival as God's stamp of approval on our status quo Christianity, we do not know that for which we pray.* In the past, awakenings brought fundamental and at times radical change. Music changed, methods emerged, both gospel proclamation and social ministry happened, and churches were planted. Revival will not affirm many of our preferences in the Christian subculture many of us cherish; it will explode them.

3. *That being said, we should pray for revival,*

starting with our own hearts. I know I am experiencing a fresh touch of God when I stop confessing everyone else's sins and start with my own. I am less concerned about what is said by a person on social media and more concerned with what the Spirit is saying to me.

4. *We should pray for revival because of Biblical teaching.* Psalm 85:6 and Habakkuk 3:2, among others, offer examples of revival prayer. Don't let the fact that these passages are in the Old Testament keep you from obeying all of Scripture! Paul calling the Roman church to be awakened (Romans 13:11-14) and our Lord calling the church at Ephesus to repent (Revelation 2) offer examples of the need to constantly seek the Lord.

5. *We pray for revival because of our study of history.* I'm far more interested in the opinions of those from history whose lives have endured as examples of godly leadership than contemporary spokesmen—including myself—who will likely fade into historical obscurity. Note these quotes from great men of God on prayer:

—*"It is God's will through His wonderful grace, that the prayers of His saints should be one of the great principal means of carrying on the designs of Christ's kingdom in the world. When God has something very great to accomplish for His church, it is His will that there should precede it the extraordinary prayers of His people; as is manifest by Ezekiel 36:37. And it is revealed that, when God is about to accomplish great things for His church, He will begin by remarkably pouring out the spirit of grace and supplication (see Zechariah 12:10)."* Jonathan Edwards, *Some Thoughts on Revival*

—*"Oh! Men and brethren, what would this heart feel if I could but believe that there were some among you who would go home and pray for a revival: men whose faith is large enough, and their love fiery enough to lead them from this moment to exercise unceasing intercessions that God would appear among us and do wondrous things here, as in the times of former generations."* Charles Spurgeon

―*"When did you last hear anyone praying for revival, praying that God might open the windows of heaven and pour out His Spirit? When did you last pray for that yourself? I suggest seriously that we are neglecting this almost entirely. We are guilty of forgetting the authority of the Holy Spirit. We are so interested in ourselves and in our own activities that we have forgotten the one thing that can make us effective. By all means let us continue to pray for the particular efforts, for the minister, and his preaching every Sunday, for all essential organizations and for evangelistic campaigns, if we feel led to have them. But before it all, and after it all, let us pray and plead for revival. When God sends revival He can do more in a single day than in fifty years of all our organization. That is the verdict of sheer history which emerges clearly from the long story of the Church."* D. Martin Lloyd-Jones

――*"I continue to dream and pray about a revival of holiness in our day that moves forth in mission and creates authentic community in which each person can be unleashed through the empowerment of the Spirit to fulfill God's creational intentions."* John Wesley

―*"When God intends great mercy for his people, he first of all sets them praying."* Matthew Henry

There is a lot of talk about revival on social media today. It could be that reading over our own social media timelines will be evidence enough to demonstrate how much we must pray for God to move in our hearts. May we talk to God more than we talk to each other about revival.

WHEN REVIVAL COMES, WE MOVE FROM A MINIMALISTIC CHRISTIANITY TO A TOTAL ABANDONMENT TO CHRIST

One of the ways we can see the need for a fresh touch of God is this: so much of Christianity in America today is of the minimalistic, add-on variety. In other words, we see so many professing Christians who in practice add Jesus to a long list of commitments, reducing our devotion to Christ to the path of least resistance and the most minimal of commitments. In her recounting of the largest study of youth and religious beliefs (the National Study of Youth and Religion or NSYR), Kenda Dean offers a scathing critique of much of church culture today and its impact on the younger generation. She writes:

> After two and a half centuries of shacking up with "the American dream," churches have perfected a dicey codependence between consumer-driven therapeutic individualism and religious pragmatism. These theological proxies gnaw, termite-like, at our identity as the Body of Christ, eroding our ability to recognize that Jesus' life of self-giving love directly challenges the American gospel of self-fulfillment and self-actualization.[2]

Dawn continues: "Churches seem to have offered teenagers a kind of 'diner theology': a bargain religion, cheap but satisfying, whose gods require little in the way of fidelity or sacrifice." Then, without using the term "revival," she describes the reason many of our churches and youth miss the very thing described throughout this book:

> The problem does not seem to be that churches are teaching young people badly, but that *we are doing an exceedingly good job of teaching youth what we really believe: namely, that Christianity is not a big deal, that God requires little, and the church is a helpful social institution filled with nice people focused primarily on "folks like us"—which, of course, begs the question of whether we are really the church at all.*[3]

Revival shatters such ideas about Christianity, beckoning a younger generation to a more radical devotion to Christ. John and I saw this in our early years in the Jesus Movement, and again in this movement. Young people long for this, but most need to hear the stories of revival to begin to understand what they have not yet seen.

Part of our need for a God-movement relates to wider cultural influences. If you go back a century or so you can observe the rise of factories as cities grew and the Industrial Revolution took hold. People in increasing numbers worked in factories, leading to the rise of the 40 hour work week, labor unions to protect workers, even while an increasingly prosperous America gave people a heightened interest in leisure as seen in such things as the push toward more vacation time and slogans like TGIF (Thank God It's Friday). The job became for many a means to a greater end, such as leisure time and early retirement. The unintended consequence of this was a mindset of punch-in, do what you have to do, and punch-out of the job.

This mindset has become prevalent in the church today. So many people attending on Sundays functionally see their faith as this: as long as I show up regularly, give a little money, and serve in some way, I am a great Christian. This is minimalistic Christianity and a stunted form of what God created us for. But when revival comes all that changes.

When God moves on believers, we no longer consider how little we can do to get by, but we earnestly seek to surrender everything to Christ. This leads to a holistic way of looking at life where following Jesus is not a Sunday event primarily but is a daily walk affecting all of life. An obvious way this emerges is through new ministries of evangelism and church planting, but also through ministries of social justice. Caring for orphans has often marked revival movements as much as church planting. George Whitefield built the orphanage Bethesda, "house of mercy," because his view of the gospel did not separate his compassion for people from his proclamation of the Word. It was in fact the largest building project in the colony of Georgia at its time, and it still operates today. Francke the Pietist began an orphanage at Halle in the early 1700s, and led other social reforms while preaching Christ. Spurgeon established an orphanage, as well. John Wesley had a great impact on Wilberforce and the abolition of slavery movement. The Wesley's and Whitefield had visited the prisons regularly while in the Holy Club at Oxford. Prison reformer John Howard was encouraged by John Wesley in his efforts to bring about a change in the dreadful prisons in England and around Europe. Wesley also set up schools to educate children, focusing on evangelism. One of the effects of this awakening was its impact on Robert Raikes and the Sunday school movement. "Without doubt," said Taylor, "this was one of the major streams of evangelical power to flow from the great revival."[38] John Richard Green wrote:

> [The revival sought] to remedy the guilt, the ignorance, the physical suffering, and the social degradation of the profligate and the poor. It was not till the Wesleyan impulse had done its work that this philanthropic impulse began. The Sunday Schools established by Mr. Raikes of Gloucester at the close of the century were the beginnings of popular education. Human sympathy with the wronged and afflicted raised hospitals, endowed charities, built churches, sent missionaries to the heathen, and Wilberforce in their crusade against the iniquity of the slave-trade.[4]

If we see revival, it will not be contained in a church building; it will affect all of life.

Notes:

1. This quote, and much of the material for this chapter, was originally published in Malcolm McDow and Alvin L. Reid, *Firefall 2.0* (Wake Forest: Gospel Advance Books, 2014), p. 169f.

2. Kenda Creasy Dean, *Almost Christian : What the Faith of Our Teenagers is Telling the American Church* (Oxford University Press, 2010, Kindle Edition), location 123.

3. Ibid., location 237. Italics added.

4. Beardsley, *Religious Progress through Religious Revivals*, pp. 24-25. Cited in *Firefall 2.0*, p. 188.

CONCLUSION
A RIDICULOUS AND
REASONABLE HOPE

JOHN AVANT

A few years ago I was in Germany meeting with some missionary friends. I had a little free time and was close to the city of Worms. I decided to visit and see the monument to Martin Luther. In April of 1521, Luther stood before the Diet of Worms and refused to recant his views with the now famous words, "Here I stand. I can do no other." And the Reformation was on! There aren't too many events in history as important as the Protestant Reformation. Martin Luther is certainly one of the most important figures in that history, and indeed in all of history itself. So I was a little perplexed that I had a hard time finding anyone in Worms who had heard of him!

When I arrived in the city I couldn't find the Luther Monument. I started asking people who spoke English if they knew where it was. Over and over the answer I got was, "Who is Martin Luther?" Finally one very old person smiled and pointed me in the right direction.

It's astonishing that the very memory of the most important spiritual moments in the history of our world has been forgotten by so many. The same thing holds true of the spiritual awakenings of history. There is a very real danger that an entire generation of Christians are losing the knowledge of the history of the revivals that have shaped everything we are as evangelicals today.

Even the spiritual meaning of the word "revive" seems to have been largely lost to the world. *Dictionary.com* lists 14 meanings for the word "revive." None of them have anything to do with the historical or spiritual meaning of revival!

And then there is the complete collapse in our culture of any sense of biblical values or worldview. The very actions, behaviors and beliefs which once characterized a person as a man or woman of integrity and moral strength are now viewed as signs of bigotry and intolerance. This has happened in a stunningly brief period of time.

When you combine the contemporary ignorance of historical revival with the collapsing culture around us, the very idea of a revival that could transform culture the way that past awakenings have seems almost ridiculous. But viewed through the lens of history and of the Spirit of God's activity, this hope may not be ridiculous at all.

We see the possibility of revival in our day as a ridiculous and reasonable hope!

First of all, all of the great spiritual awakenings have been birthed in the midst of dark days. The great teacher of evangelism and revival Roy Fish always taught us: "Revival is like the tide. When it is fully out, that is the moment it begins to rush back in!"

We also see for the first time in years, a fresh focus on the need for national revival from some of the most strategic Christian leaders in America. Ronnie Floyd for instance, the President of the Southern Baptist Convention, has made this the theme of his presidency and the call of his heart to the largest evangelical denomination in the world, and to the greater body of Christ as well. Hear his heart-cry for revival:

MY PLEA

There is no great movement of God that has ever occurred that does not begin with the extraordinary prayer of God's people. The time is now for us to come together before God in clear agreement, visible union, and in extraordinary prayer for the next Great Awakening and for the world to be reached for Christ.

For the sake of our nation and the spiritually lost around the world, it is time to humble ourselves before God. For this, I plead with all Southern Baptist pastors, missionaries, laypersons, denominational leaders, churches, denominational entities, conventions, colleges and universities; from student to adult, regardless of age, vocation, or status.

As we come to God in humility and repentance, entering into this special season of extraordinary prayer, we plead with God for spiritual revival personally, revival in the church, and the next Great Awakening in the United States. As Martyn Lloyd-Jones writes:

"And in movements of the Spirit the first thing that happens and which eventually leads to a great revival is that one man or a group of men suddenly begin to feel this burden and they feel the burden so much that they are led to do something about it."
(Revival: *Martyn Lloyd-Jones, p. 163)*

I am pleading with each of you to join in this spiritual movement to pray for the next Great Awakening so the Great Commission will escalate to its rightful priority and accelerate to its completion in our generation.

A LOOK BACK

Jonathan Edwards was a man who believed in the

absolute sovereignty of God. He was the catalyst for the first Great Awakening and was even impactful in the second Great Awakening. Even with Edwards' deep abiding belief in God's sovereignty, he called upon God's people to act because he believed God would listen to the promptings of His people.

In fact, in Malcolm McDow and Alvin L. Reid's **Firefall 2.0: How God Shapes History Through Revival** *(Wake Forest: Gospel Advance Books, 2014), p. 207, they record the words that Edwards wrote to pastors directly:*

> *Be much in prayer and fasting, both in secret and with one another. It seems to me, it would become the circumstances of the present day, if ministers in a neighborhood would often meet together, and spend days in fasting and fervent prayer among themselves.... So it is God's will that the prayers of His saints shall be great and the principal means of carrying on the designs of Christ's Kingdom in the world. When God has something to accomplish for His church, it is with His will that there should precede it the extraordinary prayer of His people.*

Therefore, as we look back, we must fully embrace the deep belief that God responds to the prayers of His people, especially when these prayers are cried out to Him in desperation and done in an extraordinary way. Evidence is becoming clearer nationally that God is calling His people into a season of special focus and commitment to extraordinary prayer.

*It has been over 100 years since the last great move of God occurred in our nation. It was in 1857 and 1858 that a movement of prayer led to **1 million people becoming Christ-followers** from a population of only 30* *million in our nation. This movement of prayer was begun in New York City by a layperson named Jeremiah Lanphier. After failing to minister effectively to the immigrants in his church's neighborhood, Lanphier was moved to pray.*

At noon on September 23, 1857, in the Dutch Reformed Church on Fulton Street in New York City, Jeremiah Lanphier knelt alone. Before 1 p.m. six men joined him. Within a month, 100 men joined him daily. Soon, thousands of men began to pray each day at noon around New York City. This resulted in 1 million Americans coming to Christ within a two-year span, as well as another 1 million converted to Christ in Great Britain and Ireland. The church was revived. Christians were never the same. The fires of evangelism were burning brightly. The advance of the gospel to the nations of the world was profound. Men like David Livingstone, J. Hudson Taylor, and eventually the Student Volunteer Movement saw 20,000 young people surrender their lives to missions. Additionally, these great movements of God impacted renowned men of history like Charles Spurgeon, D. L. Moody, and William Booth.

These were not perfect times. Simultaneously, tension over slavery was growing and financial panic was occurring. In this time of uncertainty, God's people became desperate and began to cry out to Him. The Sovereign God of Heaven determined to pour out His Spirit in a supernatural way, resulting in one of the greatest movements of God in the history of our nation.

While it has been over 100 years since the last great movement of God upon our nation, we cannot ignore the moments when the Lord has still moved upon our nation powerfully. For example, in the early 1970s, the Jesus Movement touched a generation, including many of our leaders today. **Through this work of God, thousands came to Christ, followed by many of them being called into ministry.** *The greatest year of reaching and baptizing teenagers in our Southern Baptist history occurred in 1972, all due to the influence of the Jesus Movement. While not a "great" awakening, many joyfully remember the work of God in those days.*

Sadly, we now have a generation or more of people who have never experienced anything close to a movement of God with this level of impact. It is past time for this to change. God is ready, are we?

OUR PRESENT STATUS

Unquestionably, we find ourselves experiencing days unlike any we have seen in our history. The moral slide in our nation has degraded into a revolution that seems to be out of control. While marriage is being redefined by our culture and the family is under an unprecedented attack, social problems are rising everywhere due to this new cultural reality. Simultaneously, there are so many national and global crises rising up that we cannot keep up with their supposed threats. As well, the world is becoming more dangerous by the second.

While this present status is undeniable, much of the church in America sleeps. Spiritual lukewarmness is plaguing the church, resulting in the infrequency of church attendance, declining churches, lagging evangelism, sagging giving, and generational disconnectedness. Complacency and conflict categorize the church more than contrition and compassion. Among the people of God, announcements and promotions within the church gain a higher priority in planning and follow through than prayer.

While these realities are rising to a seeming point of no return, it is in this hour that we must wake up from our slothfulness and sleep. Romans 13:11 says, "Besides this, knowing the time, it is already the hour for you to wake up from sleep, for now our salvation is nearer than when we first believed."

We are at a decisive point in time. Therefore, this is an undeniable moment and season, fixed by a sovereign God as a moment of destiny. God is at work and we cannot miss this season of decision and opportunity by being unresponsive and asleep.

A CALL TO EXTRAORDINARY PRAYER AND URGENT ACTION

The church must rise up in extraordinary prayer and urgent action. We must take desperate steps forward spiritually during these desperate times in which we live. With urgency in this hour, knowing the Lord could return at anytime, it is incumbent on us to rise up together now as His Church.

Therefore, I am pleading with our Southern Baptist Family to come together in clear agreement, visible union, and extraordinary prayer for the next Great Awakening and for the world to be reached for Christ.

*Recently, I read a **sermon** by Dr. Billy Graham that he preached on October 14, 1993, at the Southern Baptist Theological Seminary. In this sermon, "**Can Revival Come?**", Dr. Graham called for revival and awakening. In one sentence, he cast a vision that represents my overwhelming passion personally and for* *all Southern Baptists. He said,*

> *"An awakening can bring about evangelization of the world in our generation."*

These words so resonate with my pleading with Southern Baptists and beyond.

Surely we can embrace with clear agreement that spiritual revival personally, spiritual revival in the church, and spiritual awakening in the nation are all needed so we can accelerate our pace in reaching the world for Christ. Certainly we can deny ourselves, defer our own preferences, and visibly unite in extraordinary prayer for the next Great Awakening and for the world to be reached for Christ.

And so this hope of revival is real. It is grounded in real history, in the real Word of God and in the real prayers and all-in focus of key Kingdom leaders all over the world.

Even the secular world is longing for revival—they just don't know what to call it. When people swim in a cesspool long enough they just can't help but begin to wonder if there is something pure, something clean and refreshing they are missing somewhere. And they are beginning to look, all around us, for that clear water, with a certain sense of desperation.

An entire generation is hungry for hope, security and meaning. According to Amazon, the most highlighted passage of *all* books on Kindle is from the second book in the *Hunger Games* series:

"Because sometimes things happen to people and they're not equipped to deal with them."

Do you hear the heart-cry for hope in this? Professor Mark Shiffman comments on this passage:

It's easy to see why *The Hunger Games* is the novel [of a] generation. The trilogy depicts adolescents rigorously trained by adults for desperate but meaningless life-or-death competitions. [The story] resonates with students'...worry that they're all honed up with no place to go...They rack up majors, minors, certificates, credentials, and internships to keep them in the running for what they feel to be an ever more elusive success. They're driven by fear...They clothe themselves in an armor of achievement that they hope will protect them against uncertainties...also the deeper uncertainties about their status, their identities, their self-worth...[They are trying to gain] more control over an uncertain future.[1]

Wow.

We have the answer to their search. We have The Gospel! Revival is the wind-driven viral fire that can sweep through a generation with the gospel-centered answers to these deep questions and longings.

So what can we do to make this hope of revival more reasonable and less ridiculous? Here are a few humble suggestions.

PRAY LIKE THE DESPERATE

Have you ever seen desperate people pray? Have you been one? When your baby is desperately sick, when your son is clinging to life after an accident, when you have just heard a dread diagnosis, you pray differently. You pray like nothing else matters because, well, nothing else really does. It's time for a renewal of serious prayer gatherings. Pastors must pray together again and lead their churches to join hands for revival. You and I must pray like desperate people.

Pray desperate prayers like Moses who can't imagine living or leading people forward without the presence and glory of God. He gets bold with God and says, "If your presence will not go with me do not bring us up from here. For how shall it be known that I have found favor in your sight, I and your people? Is it not in your going with us, so that we are distinct, I and your people, from every other people on the face of the earth?" (Exodus 33:16) And God answers! "This very thing that you have spoken I will do, for you have found favor in my sight and I know you by name." (Exodus 33:17) But that still wasn't enough for Moses. He was desperate. He wanted more. He needed more. "Please show me your glory," he says. (Exodus 33:18) We need it as much as Moses did. So let's ask for it. In the last chapter Alvin clearly presented the truth that "when revival comes, prayer matters more than ever." It also matters more than ever so that revival *will* come!

CONNECT REVIVAL HISTORY TO PRESENT HUNGER

We simply must teach the history of what God has done in the world. Imagine understanding who America is as a nation if we had no knowledge of the Revolutionary war, the Civil War or heroic leaders like Washington and Lincoln. If the Church loses even the basic history of Awakening we will lose the knowledge of who we really are at our Spirit-filled best.

But don't just teach history classes. Teach present and powerful possibilities! Teach how a movement like the First Great Awakening could address the fear and uncertainty about the condition of our nation. Teach how a businessman, not a pastor, could be used to spark a movement that reaches a million people in a year, like what happened through Jeremiah Lanphier in 1858. Teach how one young person could shape her entire generation, even see social injustices change in an entire nation, as happened through Florrie Evans in Wales in 1904. Teach revival as the historically proven answer to the longings of every heart in our day.

There has never been a time in history when revival could spread as rapidly as it could today. Think of the time it took 200 years ago for word to spread of how God was working in the Great Awakenings. Today through the power of social media we can "tell the mighty deeds of god" (Psalm 145:6) instantly to the world! In Acts 2:11 the peoples of the nations heard in their own tongues "the mighty deeds of God." Today we could see a fresh Pentecost instantly if god moves again in power! Let's tell the stories of revival of the past and prepare to tell the new stories of his mighty deeds to the world. What a wonderful hope!

CULTIVATE GENERATIONAL CONNECTIONS

The generational divide in the Church has been devastating to church health and growth for so long. Most churches have become either very young and growing or very old and declining. But what if that could change? What if we could see churches thriving multi-generationally? What if we could see the passion and energy of youth merge with the wisdom and experience of age? We may have that opportunity before us in a way we have not seen in a long time.

Recently *Relevant* Magazine published an article

by Seth Tower Hurd entitled "Unexpected Things Millennials Want in Church." Hurd comments on the recent study by the Barna Group on Millennials and the Church. He says, "Adults in the 18-30s range are often drawn to church out of the desire to connect with those with more life wisdom."[2] This is extraordinarily good news! If we will take it, there is an opportunity before us to see new life instilled in our older generation in our churches as they find their purpose not in their own preferences but in mentoring the next generation to be "the revival generation." This could be revolutionary change and provide the needed healthy church channels for movements to begin and spread.

LEAD AS THOSE WITH NOTHING TO LOSE AND EVERYTHING TO GAIN

Churches will either change or die. Period. The kind of changes that will lead to revival movements and exponential growth and evangelism in our churches will not come easily. But what is the alternative? More churches will simply go away as they are doing now in massive numbers.

About 77 churches in North America have their final service every week.

That's 4000 churches against whom the gates of hell prevail every year. Somewhere along the line they simply ceased to exist as authentic churches and they lost their passion, their power, their mission and then their very existence.

Isn't the hour desperate enough for us to lead our churches toward something different? Toward a mission centered around the gospel and not on us? What do we have to lose?

God is calling out courageous leaders—pastors and people who will join hands and pursue God all-in to see gospel transformation—revival—come in their churches. Let's be those leaders. Let's call our churches to believe and embody the radical message of Jesus.

Let's believe and teach the gospel again for each life—the truth of 1 Timothy 6:19 that it is not the pursuit of wealth or pleasure that will bring real life but the pursuit of a grace-giving, love-pouring, awe-inspiring God that allows us to "take hold of the life that is truly life." Let's teach and model the optimistic, joyful community of hope that is the Church when she is immersed in the gospel.

Let's believe and teach the gospel again that will transform lives, challenge injustice and break the chains in evil's foulest places. A generation is rising up looking for a movement that will break the curse of sex trafficking, that will provide transformational hope to the poor that will hold the orphan and the widow with life-changing love. *Let the Church be that Movement!*

I stood at the grave of my father in June of 2013. I will never be "over" the death of this great man. But I will also never be over his life. His life verse was Micah 6:8. "He has told you, O man what is good, and what does the Lord require of you but to do justice, and to love kindness, and to walk humbly with your God?" I was one of the blessed ones who had a father who lived that verse before me. Now I want to see in my lifetime, with my eyes, what could happen when God's people, in a community called the Church, begin to live it together.

When Micah spoke these words something amazing happened. The people actually listened and began to obey–to live out justice and kindness and humility. And revival came under King Hezekiah.

And the nation was saved for 150 years!

Revival matters. Let's live and lead like it does. And just maybe we will see a movement that will save us for many years too. Even more significantly we will see a movement that affects eternity.

This is our ridiculous and reasonable hope.

Notes:

1. Mark Shiffman, "Majoring in Fear," *First Things*, posted November 10, 2014.
2. Seth Tower Hurd, "Unexpected Things Millennials Want in Church." *Relevant*, November 7, 2014.

A FINAL WORD

JOHN AVANT

Do you remember a time when you felt so close to Jesus that it was like inhaling Him with every breath and serving and sharing His love was as natural as exhaling? Has it been a while since you felt that way?

Then maybe you need revival. Just maybe God is wanting to use you to make a Kingdom difference as He has used so many others.

But maybe He is waiting on you. Waiting to see if you are ready for Him. If you really want Him. All of Him.

The Brownwood Revival was a remarkable season of life. But it is 20 years in the past. Or is it?

One of the students who was a leader on campus during the Brownwood revival is now a missionary to the Muslim world. We have called him Jay. His passion for mission was birthed during the revival years when he went with our church on a mission trip to Belarus. During that trip we had an invitation to hold a service in a 3000 seat Opera Hall. It was an amazing opportunity! But when we arrived we found that there had been no publicity done at all. So we stood outside as people got off the subway and the buses and invited them in. I speak a little Russian and I shouted over and over again inviting people in. And they came. And came. And came.

When we preached to the thousands who gathered many came forward to accept Christ. Jay's job was to distribute Bibles to those who had been saved.

Fast forward to the present day.

Jay called me from the mission field and told me he had a story to tell me. He had been surprised to find out that two young Belarussian women had come to the country where he was serving also to serve as missionaries. He sought them out to hear their stories. They told him the miracle that had led them to Jesus.

When they were very young their mother got off public transportation in Minsk one day with a friend. They were surprised to hear an American preacher mangling the Russian language and inviting them into an Opera Hall. They went in. That night their mother did not meet Jesus. But her friend did. And a college student gave her a Bible. When she got home she put the Bible beside her phone. Their mother did not have a phone so every time she would go to her friend's house to use hers she would see that Bible. And she would read it. When she finally reached the end she found there God's plan of salvation written and beckoning to her. She met Jesus then. And later led her daughters to as well. And now they were taking the message that changed their lives to the nations.

And of course, Jay was the student that gave their mother's friend that Bible!

Do you see?

The Brownwood revival is still reviving!

That's how revival works. And revival could be revived in you too. Today. Why not? Do you think God is stingy?! He is ready to move. He is wanting to move. He *will* move! In you. In me. In *us*—His Church. We believe He will. And soon. And so we humbly ask you—
—join us. Pray with us. Move with us.

Until we see—together—revival revived.

AFTERWORD

BILL BRIGHT
(1921-2003)

You are among the few in this generation, if not in all of history, who have read of such a widespread movement of the Spirit of God as recorded in this book. No book has so blessed me and encouraged me more to believe God for revival and the world.

Again and again I was moved to tears of joy and rejoicing over this fresh and exciting report of what God is doing in the lives of multitudes of students on scores of campuses and among older adults in hundreds of churches. Only God knows the number and actual extent of the current revival.

Since our Lord Jesus came "to seek and to save the lost" and has commanded all of His followers to give priority to "seeking and saving the lost," I anticipate that there will be a great spiritual worldwide harvest as a result of God s mighty presence. This is what revival is all about—a personal visit from the One who loves us, who died for us, who was raised for us, who intercedes for us, and who now lives within us. Every personal encounter with our wonderful Savior brings the invitation, "Follow Me and I will make you fishers of men."

As a result of this present movement of God's Spirit, everyone whom God touches in revival power needs to pass on that
experience to another. I prayerfully believe this movement will continue to spread to every community of

this country and ultimately throughout the world. Whenever any Christian whose heart is ignited with the fire of heaven comes in touch with one whose heart is hungry for God but presently living in spiritual defeat, another fire will be ignited. In like manner, every believer awakened in Christ will want to be involved as Paul described in Colossians 1:28: "Everywhere we go we talk about Christ to all who will listen" (TLB). Personal evangelism is always the direct result of genuine personal revival.

How may we test the authenticity of what is now happening? By our spiritually enriched lives and by our burden to take the gospel to every person—beginning in our homes, churches, and communities.

One prelude to the current revival movement has been the accelerated and unprecedented movement of prayers worldwide. God is hearing the prayers of millions of His children around the world. Revival begins with prayer and results in evangelism.

My burden for revival has increased greatly over the years. As a result, God impressed me to fast and pray. He led me to pray for revival for America and the entire world and for the fulfillment of the Great Commission. Those were the most meaningful, rich, and rewarding forty days of my life. God gave me the great assurance that a mighty spiritual awakening would sweep our nation and encircle the globe, and that the greatest spiritual harvest of the centuries would follow, resulting in the fulfillment of the Great Commission.

CONTRIBUTORS

John Avant is pastor of the First Baptist Church of Concord in Knoxville TN. He holds degrees from Baylor University and Southwestern Baptist Theological Seminary (M.Div. and the Ph.D. in evangelism). He is also author of *The Passion Principle* (Mulnomah), *Authentic Power* (Multnomah), and *If God Were Real* (Simon & Shuster).

Timothy K. Beougher is Assistant Professor of Evangelism at Wheaton Graduate School and Associate Director of the Institute of Evangelism at the Billy Graham Center. He holds the M.Div. from Southwestern Baptist Theological Seminary, and the Th.M. and Ph.D. in Historical Theology from Trinity Evangelical Divinity School. Beougher is co-editor *of Evangelism for a Changing World* and author of *Richard Baxter and Conversion.*

Henry Blackaby served as Director of the Office of Prayer and Spiritual Awakening at the Home Mission Board of the Southern Baptist Convention. He has written a number of books including coauthoring with Claude V. King of *Experiencing God* and *Fresh Encounter.*

Bill Bright (1921-2003) was Founder and President of Campus Crusade for Christ International and author of forty books including *The Coming Revival: America's Call to Fast, Pray, and "Seek God's Face"* (NewLife Publications, 1995).

Dan R. Crawford taught at Southwestern Baptist Theological Seminary. He is author or compiler of multiple books, including *Where One Is Gathered in His Name* and *Night of Tragedy, Dawning of Light.* He is a former pastor, campus minister, and evangelism consultant.

Roy Fish served as Distinguished Professor of Evangelism at Southwestern Baptist Theological Seminary. He holds degrees from University of Arkansas and Southwestern Baptist Theological Seminary (Th.D.) He passed away in 2012, but will be remembered as a beloved professor, preacher and speaker who taught evangelism to more seminarians than any other professor to date.

Malcolm McDow served as Professor of Evangelism, Southwestern Baptist Theological Seminary. He holds degrees from Baylor University, Southwestern Baptist Theological Seminary, and New Orleans Baptist Theological Seminary (Th.D), and has done further studies at the Universities of Edinburgh and Oxford. He has contributed to numerous journals, magazines, and devotional publications, including co-authoring *Firefall 2.0*.

Brandi Maguire Parrish is a Communications graduate from Howard Payne University in Brownwood, Texas. Brandi hails originally from Houston, Texas. She and her husband Kelli, also noted in this book, are planting a church in Colorado.

Doug Munton is pastor of the First Baptist Church of O'Fallon, Illinois. He holds degrees from Wheaton College (B.A.) and Southwestern Baptist Theological Seminary (M.Div., Ph.D.). He is author of *Immersed: 40 Days to a Deeper Faith, Warriors in Hiding* and *Seven Steps to Becoming a Healthy Christian Leader* and has contributed to *Evangelism for a Changing World*.

Alvin L. Reid is Professor of Evangelism and Student Ministry at Southeastern Baptist Theological Seminary where he holds the Bailey Smith Chair of Evangelism. Reid previously served as the John Bisagno Chair of Evangelism at Houston Baptist University. He earned his M.Div. and Ph.D. from Southwestern Baptist Theological Seminary. He has written or edited some 20 books including *As You Go* (NavPress), *Evangelism Handbook* (B & H), and co-authoring *Firefall 2.0*.

Matt Yarrington graduated with his undergraduate degree in Christian Education and earned his Master of Arts in Evangelism at Wheaton College. He served as Student Chair of World Christian Fellowship at Wheaton.

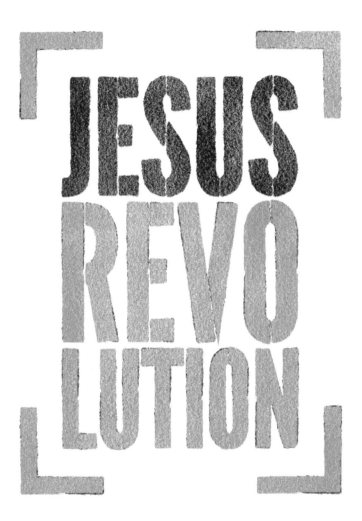

A documentary about why Jesus made the cover of
TIME Magazine in June, 1971. The true story of
America's last Great Awakening.

COMING 2015
www.thejesusrevolution.com
#JESUSREVOLUTION

Made in the USA
Middletown, DE
28 January 2020